Brother Swaggart, Why Doesn't The Cross Work For Me?

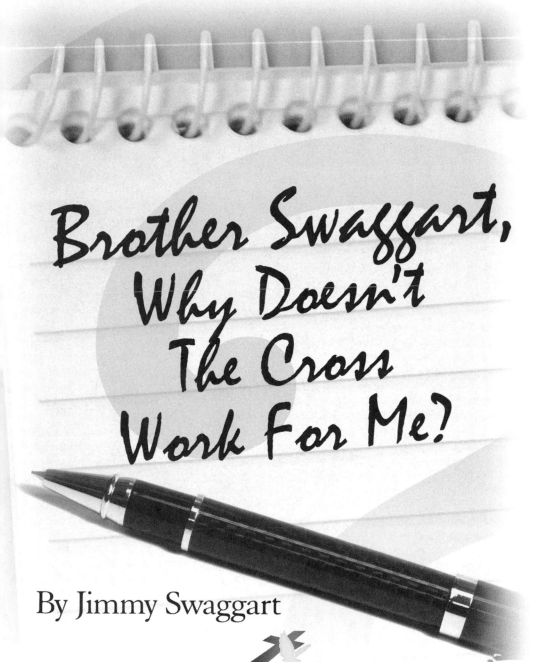

Brother Swaggart, Why Doesn't The Cross Work For Me?

By Jimmy Swaggart

JIMMY SWAGGART MINISTRIES
P.O. Box 262550 | Baton Rouge, Louisiana 70826-2550
Website: www.jsm.org | Email: info@jsm.org | Phone: 225.768.7000

ISBN 978-1-941403-05-1

09-127 | COPYRIGHT © 2014 Jimmy Swaggart Ministries®

15 16 17 18 19 20 21 22 23 / CW / 10 9 8 7 6 5 4 3 2 1

TABLE OF CONTENTS

Brother Swaggart, Why Doesn't The Cross Work For Me?

INTRODUCTION

IN 1997, THE Lord began to open up to me the great Message of the Cross. To be sure, it was not something new but is actually the oldest doctrine known to man.

Peter said: *"Forasmuch as you know that you were not redeemed with corruptible things as silver and gold, from your vain conversation* (vain lifestyle) *received by tradition from your fathers* (speaks of original sin that is passed on from father to child at conception);

"But with the precious blood of Christ (presents the payment, which proclaims the poured out life of Christ on behalf of sinners), *as of a lamb without blemish and without spot* (speaks of the lambs offered as substitutes in the old Jewish economy; the death of Christ was not an execution, an assassination, an incident or an accident, it was a sacrifice; the offering of Himself presented a perfect sacrifice, for He was perfect in every respect [Ex. 12:5]):

"Who verily was foreordained before the foundation of the world (refers to the fact that God, in His omniscience,

knew He would create man, man would fall, and man would be redeemed by Christ going to the Cross; this was all done before the universe was created; this means the Cross of Christ is the foundation doctrine of all doctrine, referring to the fact that all doctrine must be built upon that foundation, or else it is specious), *but was manifest in these last times for you* (refers to the invisible God, who, in the person of the Son, was made visible to human eyesight by assuming a human body and human limitations)" (I Pet. 1:18-20).

Of course, the full meaning of all of this was given to the Apostle Paul. One can say that Jesus is the new covenant, which means that this is far more than Christ merely having the new covenant, but rather He is the new covenant. However, the meaning of this new covenant was given to the Apostle Paul, the meaning of which in totality is the Cross of Christ.

THE JOY OF MY HEART

The first thing the Lord showed me was the meaning of the *"sin nature."* Actually, that particular morning before daylight, I was in the office studying Chapter 6 of Romans. In my study, I picked up a book by the Greek scholar, Dr. Kenneth Wuest, and turned to the particular verse in question and began to read. I suppose I had read these very passages previously, but somehow, the meaning of these passages did not register on me.

Wuest began to explain the sin nature, what it is, how it affects the believer, etc. The Holy Spirit opened up my heart to understand this tremendous doctrine regarding why the believer fails. Now, why we as believers, who love the Lord very much and who abhor sin, but yet, fail, is very critical. Most of the time, the reason is because the believer does not understand the sin nature.

I had seen the term before but had never really read anything about it that explained what it was. However, the Lord opened it up to me that morning. I found myself pacing across the floor with tears rolling down my face, thanking the Lord for the tremendous degree of information that He had imparted to me. Even though the Lord did not give me the solution to the problem at that time, the knowledge of knowing why something has happened, when before I had drawn a blank, was to me a tremendously important situation. Now I knew why the failure!

Now, don't misunderstand. Failure on the part of the Christian is always the fault of the Christian. It's certainly not the fault of God. It is always and without exception the fault of the believer, but the reason for the failure is far different than most people think. Most of the time, the failure is merely a symptom of the real problem, and the real problem is not fully understanding the sin nature.

THE CROSS

A few weeks later in one of our morning prayer meetings, the Lord opened up to me the solution to the problem, in other words, how to have victory, and I mean total victory over the sin nature that it never raise its head as a problem anymore.

In a very simple way, with only about eight or 10 people present that particular morning, the Lord spoke to my heart and said:

- The answer for which you seek is found in the Cross.

Then the Lord said it the second time, with a slight change:

- The solution for which you seek is found in the Cross.

And then, the third time came, but with a startling revelation. He said:

- The answer for which you seek is found *only* in the Cross.

In this, He once again took me back to Chapter 6 of Romans. He showed me how the believer died with Christ, was buried with Christ, and was resurrected with Christ to the position of a new man (Rom. 6:3-5).

I will never forget how happy that I was, with the joy of the Lord filling my soul as the Lord opened up this simple thing to me. But yet, the Lord didn't mention the Holy Spirit, at least not at that time.

THE HOLY SPIRIT

I knew the Holy Spirit played a great part in all of this, but the Lord never told me how. I was to learn a little later that this truth of how the Holy Spirit works, as the Lord would give it to me, would be one of the greatest truths that the church could ever know. Once again, it was not something new, but that which the Lord had already given to the Apostle Paul. Still, the words of the Lord resonated in my mind and spirit when He had said, *"The answer for which you seek is found only in the Cross."* While He never mentioned the Holy Spirit at that time, still, I knew that the Holy Spirit had to play a great part in some way. I was to find out very soon that the part He plays is great indeed.

HOW THE HOLY SPIRIT WORKS

Back in March 1988, at a very trying time for me personally and for the ministry, the Lord spoke something to me in the midst of all of this that was startling indeed.

That particular morning while I was in prayer, Satan had attacked very powerfully. It was so powerful, in fact, that I reminded the Lord that He had said, *"There has no temptation taken you but such as is common to man: but God is faithful, who will not suffer you to be tempted above that you are able; but will with the temptation also make a way to escape, that you may be able to bear it"* (I Cor. 10:13). I remonstrated that I felt the Lord was allowing Satan too much latitude. At any rate, the Lord heard my petition.

One moment, it was as if a thousand pounds were on my shoulders, and the next moment, the power of God moved over me to such an extent that I think I have never experienced such before or since. Then the Lord spoke to my heart. He said, *"I'm going to show you things about the Holy Spirit you do not now know."*

My thoughts instantly went to who the Holy Spirit is. Concerning that, there were all kinds of things about the Holy Spirit I did not know, nor did any other human being for that matter. But yet, I somehow knew that the Lord was speaking of the situation at hand. One moment, I was weighted down with the powers of darkness, and the next moment, it was like I was walking on clouds. But yet, as the weeks went into months, there was nothing that happened that I could say had fulfilled what the Lord had told me.

In fact, it was to be some nine years before that answer would come. Actually, the Lord told me in October 1991 to begin two prayer meetings a day, which I immediately carried out and continue unto this hour.

THE ANSWER TO MY PRAYER

The year now was 1997. Just a few weeks earlier, the Lord had given me the great word of the Cross, and now He was to do something as great or greater.

Since the Lord had begun to open up the Message of the Cross, I was attempting to teach it over our morning radio program, *A Study in the Word*. It was a program that aired Monday through Friday, which was one hour and 15 minutes in length.

Loren Larson was the only other person on the program with me that day. The program had almost ended when all of a sudden, something came out of my mouth that I had never heard, never read anything about it, did not know it, and yet, there it was.

I made the statement, *"The Holy Spirit works entirely within the parameters of the finished work of Christ and will not work outside of those parameters."*

I sat there stunned for a few moments, wondering where that came from. There was dead silence from both of us, which you don't do on radio. At any rate, Loren then spoke up and asked, *"Can you give me Scripture for that?"*

How could I give him Scripture when I didn't even know what I had said? What did it mean, *"The Holy Spirit works entirely within the parameters of the Cross of Christ and will not work outside of those parameters"*?

Then I looked down at my Bible, which was open to Romans, Chapter 8. Verse 2 leaped out at me.

"The law of the Spirit of life in Christ Jesus has made me free from the law of sin and death" (Rom. 8:2). There was the Scripture. In other words, the Lord was telling me at that moment how the Holy Spirit works. It is the Cross of Christ which gives Him the legal means to do all that He does. Since then, I've learned a lot about how the Holy Spirit works.

At any rate, the program ended a few moments later.

THE LORD SPOKE TO ME

As I stood up and turned to my right to walk out of the small studio, all of a sudden, the Spirit of God came upon me mightily, and the Lord spoke to me, saying, *"Do you remember the promise I made to you in March of 1988?"* Of course, I did!

Then the Lord said, *"I have just kept My word to you, showing you things about the Holy Spirit that you did not know."* Indeed He had.

To be very brief, all of this means that if we want the Holy Spirit to work within our lives, in which we cannot do anything without Him, our faith must be anchored exclusively in Christ and the Cross. That being done and maintained, the Holy Spirit will then work mightily within our hearts and lives. Otherwise, while He does not leave us, and thank God for that, still, we tie His hands, so to speak, when our faith is elsewhere other than the Cross. That's why Paul said:

"For the preaching of the Cross is to them who perish foolishness, but unto us who are saved it is the power of God" (I Cor. 1:18).

Is the power in the Cross itself? No, it isn't! The power is in the Holy Spirit. However, considering that the Holy Spirit works entirely within the parameters of the Cross of Christ and will not work outside of those parameters, this shows us how the Holy Spirit works. This, as stated, is one of the greatest truths in the entirety of the Word of God, but yet, almost unknown as it regards the modern church.

THE HOLY SPIRIT AND THE CROSS

Before the Cross, due to the fact that the blood of bulls and goats could not take away sins (Heb. 10:4), the Holy

Spirit could not come into the hearts and lives of believers to abide permanently. While He went into the hearts of some, such as prophets, to help them carry out their tasks, when that was ended, He left out again. Jesus said that the Holy Spirit was with believers before the Cross, but after the Cross, would be in believers (Jn. 14:17).

As we've already stated, the reason the Holy Spirit could not come into the hearts and lives of all believers before the Cross was because the blood of bulls and goats could not take away sins, meaning that the sin debt remained. However, when Jesus died on the Cross, that settled the sin debt once and for all, at least for all who will believe (Jn. 3:16).

That's what Paul was speaking about when he said, as it concerned the resurrection of Christ, that first Jesus, *"when He ascended up on high, He led captivity captive"* (Eph. 4:8).

This means that before the Cross, all the believers in paradise were actually captives of Satan. While Satan could not get them over into the burning side of hell, still, they were his captives because, as stated, the blood of bulls and goats could not take away sins.

However, when Jesus died on the Cross, He made all of those people in paradise, ever how many there were, who were captives of Satan, in effect, His captives, and there was nothing Satan could do about it. The debt was forever paid.

As well, before the Cross, when believers died, as we just stated, they did not go to heaven, but rather down into paradise. Since the Cross, due to the fact of the sin debt being settled at the Cross, whenever a believer dies, his soul and spirit instantly go to be with the Lord Jesus Christ in heaven (Phil. 1:23). I trust that one can see just how important the Cross was and is. In fact, everything hinges on the Cross. Whenever people tell us that we address the Cross too much, they simply don't know what they're talking about.

BROTHER SWAGGART, WHY DOESN'T THE CROSS WORK FOR ME?

When we began to preach the Cross strongly, which very soon graduated to television and now covers a great part of this world, I began to hear some people ask questions or make statements such as:

"Brother Swaggart, why doesn't the Cross work for me?"
"There must be something wrong with me."
"Why does it work for others and not for me?"
"I've tried the Cross, and it doesn't work."

Actually, the list is almost endless.

The truth is, oh yes, the Cross works wondrously well (Rom. 6:1-14; Col. 2:10-15). It's you and me who don't work very well, not the Cross.

At any rate, it was a Saturday night, I think. It must have been about 11 p.m. Frances and I had gone to bed. I had not yet gone to sleep, so what happened was not a dream, and neither was it a vision. At any rate, the Lord began to move upon me as it regarded this subject that we have broached and began to show me from the Word of God, actually, from the great book of Exodus, just exactly how Satan works in this respect. It was so powerful in my spirit that I got up, got a pencil and paper, and wrote down what the Lord gave me.

I want to give that to you in this volume, believing that it will help you greatly.

Actually, as we begin this book, we will deal with quite a few particulars in Moses' life before we get to the meat of the problem. So, I'm going to ask you to be patient as you read this book, for without question, we will get to that which the Lord has shown me. I think it will be a great blessing to you and will answer many, many questions.

It may seem strange for material given in the Old Testament, actually the great book of Exodus, to answer questions concerning the new covenant and this present time. However, it does!

As we have stated several times in this introduction, the Message of the Cross is not something that is new. In fact, it is the oldest doctrine known to man, actually formulated in the mind of the Godhead from before the foundation of the world (I Pet. 1:18-20). Unfortunately, the modern church is little preaching the Cross of Christ, if at all. We must understand that while Jesus Christ is the source of all things we receive from God, the Cross of Christ is the means by which all of this is made possible. As we have repeatedly stated, the Holy Spirit works entirely within the parameters of the finished work of Christ. He doesn't demand much of us, but He does demand one thing, and of that He will not relent.

He demands that our faith be exclusively in Christ and the Cross, and maintained exclusively in Christ and the Cross (Lk. 9:23).

"All my doubts I give to Jesus,
"I've His gracious promise heard:
"I shall never be confounded,
"I am trusting in that Word."

"All my sin I lay on Jesus,
"He does wash me in His blood,
"He will keep me pure and holy,
"He will bring me home to God."

"All my fears I give to Jesus,
"Rests my weary soul on Him;
"Though my way be hid in darkness,
"Never can His light grow dim."

"All my joys I give to Jesus,
"He is all I want of bliss;
"He of all the worlds is Master;
"He has all I need in this."

"All I am I give to Jesus;
"All my body, all my soul;
"All I have, and all I hope for,
"While eternal ages roll."

Israel In Bondage

ISRAEL IN BONDAGE

"Now these are the names of the children of Israel, which came into Egypt; every man and his household came with Jacob.

"Reuben, Simeon, Levi, and Judah,

"Issachar, Zebulun, and Benjamin,

"Dan, and Naphtali, Gad, and Asher.

"And all the souls that came out of the loins of Jacob were seventy souls: for Joseph was in Egypt already" (Ex. 1:1-5).

We look at Jacob's family, the 70 souls which the hand of the Lord brought from Canaan to Egypt for safekeeping, one might say. They were insignificant in the eyes of the world, but if God be in it, we must never despise the day of small things.

Joseph and his generation died, which marked the ending of one era and the beginning of another. Even though no principal individuals are recorded during the coming time, still, the ways of God continued to be taught to the people, at least after a fashion.

Because of these being God's people, they were *"fruitful, and increased abundantly, and multiplied, and waxed exceeding mighty"* (Ex. 1:7). The blessings of God are upon that which belongs to God.

THE NAMES

The book of Genesis is the story of the fall of man. The book of Exodus is the story of the redemption of man; hence, the work of redemption by Christ is called His *exodus* (deceased, going out of the world, Lk. 9:31).

Actually, the book of Exodus teaches that redemption can only be effected by blood. It opens with Israel as a helpless slave in the power of the enemy and doomed by him to destruction. That is the state of multiple millions of Christians at this present time. In Exodus, Egypt is a type of the world with all of its evil systems and, as well, ruled by the prince of darkness, Satan. The book closes with Israel redeemed, enriched, and free. All of this was effected by the death of the paschal lamb, which was a type of the coming Redeemer, who would suffer for the entirety of the world (Jn. 3:16).

The first few chapters in the book of Exodus consist of the answer to our question. If we are to notice, the book of Exodus begins with names, hence, salvation is a personal matter. We must not forget that. It means that salvation is not corporate, even though the church may be corporate.

JOSEPH

Joseph died some 140-plus years before Israel left Egypt, or some 60-plus years before Moses was born. The king who began enslaving Israel reigned during the last part of this 60-odd years, for when Moses was born, Pharaoh's policy was in force.

The conduct of Joseph's brethren against him was what ultimately brought them into Egypt; consequently, we must take two things into account:

1. We see the ugly manner in which the brothers of Joseph conducted themselves toward God.
2. We note the encouraging manner in which God conducted Himself toward the brothers of Joseph.

To be sure, their actions were overly ugly, so ugly, in fact, that they could be termed only in the realm of murder. In a sense, their acting in this manner toward Joseph was the same as them acting toward God, i.e., Christ. Jesus Himself said, *"Verily I say unto you, Inasmuch as you have done it unto one of the least of these My brethren, you have done it unto Me"* (Mat. 25:40).

THE WORD OF GOD

However, God was in all of this, and He was in it to bring good out of evil. Joseph's brothers might have sold him to the Ishmaelites, and they might have sold him to Potiphar, and Potiphar might have thrown him in prison, but God was above all of this, working out His own plans.

Concerning all of this, C.H. Mackintosh said: *"There are wheels within wheels in the government of God. He makes use of an endless variety of agencies in the accomplishment of His unsearchable designs. Potiphar's wife, Pharaoh's butler, Pharaoh's dreams, Pharaoh himself, the dungeon, the throne, the fetter, the famine—all are at His sovereign disposal, and all are made instrumental in the development of His stupendous counsels."*

As one studies the Word of God, one quickly finds that with God in the mix, the potentials are endless. Let us understand that exactly as He worked then, He also works now. There is only one requirement that He has of us, and that is faith. Someone must have faith, and in the time of the patriarchs, they were known for their faith.

THE CHILDREN OF ISRAEL

"And Joseph died, and all his brethren, and all that generation.

"And the children of Israel were fruitful, and increased abundantly, and multiplied, and waxed exceeding mighty; and the land was filled with them" (Ex. 1:6-7).

Joseph died, but God didn't die. He continued to bless the children of Israel until they grew into a mighty nation.

From the time that God called Abraham out of Ur of the Chaldees until the children of Israel were delivered from Egyptian bondage was 430 years. From the time of Abraham until the time that Jacob moved into Egypt was a period of some 215 years. So, the children of Israel actually stayed in Egypt per se for 215 years, as well, making a total of 430 years.

Why did God desire that they remain that long in this land? Why did He allow them to be reduced to slavery?

Two reasons:

1. He wanted them to grow into a mighty nation before He brought them into the Promised Land, and that they did. Actually, they would be some 3 million strong when they left Egypt.
2. He allowed them to be reduced to slavery so they would want to leave. Had they continued as they were during the time of Joseph, actually having the best of the land and being treated as royal guests, there is no way they would have left Egypt. They had to be reduced to abject slavery, and the worst kind at that, before they were ready to leave.

As someone has well said, *"Man will seldom carry out the will of God until he thinks it's in his own personal interests to do so."* That's sad but true!

THE NEW KING

"Now there arose up a new king over Egypt, which knew not Joseph" (Ex. 1:8).

We will find that the wise planning of the Egyptian monarch was very clever so long as he left God out. However, the entrance of God into these plans turned his wisdom to folly. All schemes that ignore God illustrate human fallibility, and one might say, illustrate human stupidity.

Evidently the Lord gave the children of Israel excellent health and freedom from disease.

According to accounts, as stated, the children of Israel were in Egypt 215 years. This counts from the time that Jacob came into Egypt with 70 souls until they were delivered some 215 years later.

As well, there is a good possibility that each of the sons of Jacob had a household of a number of people, perhaps even as many as 50. That being the case, it could have been as many as 2,000 people who went into Egypt.

According to some authorities, if there be no artificial check restraining it, population tends to double itself approximately every 25 years. If, in fact, there were approximately 2,000 people in this entourage, in some 215 years, according to the estimates, they would have multiplied to approximately 2 million. Considering that they were extremely healthy and that disease was not carrying them off, as it did many in those days, in the 215-year period, that number could easily have swollen to approximately 3 million people, which is the estimate concerning the number who were delivered. There were 600,000 men of war, the Scripture tells us, which wouldn't count all men above 40 years of age or those under 20. This means that there were probably well over 1 million men. There would have been at least that many adult women, besides all the children.

THE EGYPTIAN RECORDS

It has been stated by some that in the Egyptian records, there is no mention of the Hebrews as the Bible claims. However, it is known that at about the time of the Hebrew sojourn, there was in Egypt a subject race, which was often employed in forced labors, and was called *"Aperu"* or *"Aperiu."* It seems impossible to deny that this word is a very fair Egyptian equivalent for the biblical *Hebrews.* We are forced, therefore, either to suppose that there were in Egypt, at one and the same time, two subject races with names almost identical, or to admit the identification of the Aperu with the descendants of Jacob.

The exact numbers of the Aperu are nowhere mentioned. However, it is a calculation by some authorities that under Rameses II, a little before the exodus, the foreign races in Egypt amounted certainly to a third, and probably still more, of the whole population. The Aperu were beyond all doubt the chief of these foreign races. That population of Egypt was reckoned at approximately 8 million, of which a third would be a little over 2.5 million. Without a doubt, it seems obvious that the Aperu identified in the Egyptian records were indeed the Hebrews.

WHO KNEW NOT JOSEPH

It is believed that the children of Israel were delivered from Egypt at approximately 1600 B.C.

The new king mentioned here by Moses was probably either Rameses I or his son, Seti I, and then some claim it was Rameses IV, surnamed Meiamoun. It is believed that the Pharaoh who reigned when the Israelites went out of Egypt was Rameses V, named *Amenophis* or *Menephtha*. There is a disagreement over whether this particular pharaoh was Rameses II or Rameses V.

It seems that the persecution lasted for approximately 100 years. We know that it was in force when Moses was born. He spent 40 years in Egypt and 40 years, as well, at the backside of the desert. That totals 80 years in which the persecutions continued, with it probably going on some 10 to 20 years before Moses was born.

When Jacob came into Egypt, Joseph was about 38 years old. He died at 110, so it was about 60 years after his death that this new king began to reign.

When the Scripture says, *"a new king ... which knew not Joseph,"* it means he did not regard him, even though he would certainly have known the name. There is no way that this great thing could have been done in Egypt those years earlier without this Pharaoh being perfectly aware. The great thing of which we speak is what Joseph instituted as it regarded the superintending of Egypt during the time of the great harvests and the famine.

THE CHILDREN OF ISRAEL

"And he said unto his people, Behold, the people of the children of Israel are more and mightier than we" (Ex. 1:9).

This new king was very well aware of Joseph and of the children of Israel. However, because of their tremendous population and, no doubt, coupled with their industry, he was fearful of them and determined to show them no favor whatsoever. In other words, he would make slaves of them.

Most probably, the new Egyptian Pharaoh exaggerated when he spoke of the children of Israel being more and mightier, even though they were, in fact, very strong and getting stronger every day. In fact, he would use this as an excuse to institute his reforms, as he would have called them.

THE PLANS OF PHARAOH

"Come on, let us deal wisely with them; lest they multiply, and it come to pass, that, when there falls out any war, they join also unto our enemies, and fight against us, and so get them up out of the land" (Ex. 1:10).

We find in this verse an evil king (Pharaoh) who set out to destroy God's people. To be sure, his plans to do so were keen and far-reaching, at least as long as God was left out, but the entrance of God into these plans turned his wisdom to folly. All schemes that ignore God illustrate the same.

The world, not knowing God, little uses its wisdom aright. Only a few times in history record it doing such. The Pharaoh who made Joseph the prime minister of Egypt portrays one of the few times of such happening. To be frank, it would not have happened then had not God moved upon that particular monarch. Most of the time, the people of God are more or less opposed, with the world completely misjudging them.

For instance, the Pharaoh of this time passed judgment upon the Israelites and imagined all sorts of evil things. He imagined they would join Egypt's enemies, thereby, fighting against Egypt. The truth was, Israel had no such thing in mind. However, as we shall see, the evil plans fomented by Pharaoh were to be used by God, just as the righteous plans were used by God as it regarded the Pharaoh of Joseph's day. While man is limited, God is never limited unless we limit Him through unbelief. He is able to take anything and turn it to good, but He does seek cooperation by believers.

TREASURE CITIES

"Therefore they did set over them taskmasters to afflict them with their burdens. And they built for Pharaoh treasure cities, Pithom and Raamses" (Ex. 1:11).

The ruins of Pithom and Raamses exist presently, and, in fact, the latter was the residence of the court. There is a good possibility that the miracles of Moses recorded in Exodus, Chapter 7, took place in this court (Ps. 78:12, 43). So, the great palaces built by the children of God, who were used as slaves, would see the mighty power of God made evident in them.

BLESSED

"*But the more they afflicted them, the more they multiplied and grew. And they were grieved because of the children of Israel*" (Ex. 1:12).

The first phrase of this verse is interesting indeed, "*But the more they afflicted them, the more they multiplied and grew.*"

Concerning this, Mackintosh said: "*In reference to the king of Egypt, it may assuredly be said, he did 'greatly err,' not knowing God or His changeless counsels. He knew not that, hundreds of years back, before even he had breathed the breath of mortal life, God's Word and oath — 'two immutable things' — had infallibly secured the full and glorious deliverance of that very people, in fact a people which at that time, the time of the oath of God, didn't even exist, whom he was going, in his earthly wisdom, to crush. All this was unknown to him, and therefore all his thoughts and plans were founded upon ignorance of that grand foundation — truth of all truths, namely, that 'God is.' He vainly imagined that he, by his management, could prevent the increase of those concerning whom God had said, 'They shall be as the stars of heaven, and as the sand which is upon the seashore.' His wise dealing, therefore, was simply madness and folly.*"

THE MORE THEY MULTIPLIED

The idea of this phrase is, the more that Satan engineered, through Pharaoh, the persecution, the more that

God increased the blessings. One must shout *"Hallelujah!"* What God has blessed, nothing can curse. We must never forget that.

If man cooperates with God, places his faith aright in Christ and His Cross, and maintains his faith in that finished work, it really doesn't matter what Satan does. Admittedly, it may look very negative for awhile, for who would have bought stock in Job when he sat in the midst of an ash heap with everything gone? Who would have purchased stock in David when he was hiding in caves, running from Saul? Who would have purchased stock in the early church, with Caesar vowing its destruction?

However, none of that mattered. If believing man will maintain his faith in Christ and what Christ has done for him at the Cross, and not allow his faith to be moved from that work that is forever finished, ultimately, the blessings will come, and God will pour them on. The more that Pharaoh afflicted the people of God, the more that God multiplied them. *"If God be for us, who can be against us?"* (Rom. 8:31).

THE ETERNAL GOD

What a sad mistake, therefore, for a feeble mortal, no matter how powerful he might be to those around him, to set himself up against the eternal God, and as one preacher said, *"To rush against the thick bosses of the shield of the Almighty!"* As well, might the monarch have sought to stem the ocean's tide with his puny hand as to prevent the increase of those who were the subjects of Jehovah's everlasting purpose. Hence, although *"they did set over them taskmasters to afflict them with their burdens,"* yet, *"the more they afflicted them, the more they multiplied and grew."* Thus it must ever be. *"He who sits in the heavens shall laugh: the* LORD *shall have them in derision"* (Ps. 2:4). Eternal confusion shall be inscribed upon all the opposition of men and demons.

THE EGYPTIANS

"And the Egyptians made the children of Israel to serve with rigor:

"And they made their lives bitter with hard bondage, in mortar, and in brick, and in all manner of service in the field: all their service, wherein they made them serve, was with rigor" (Ex. 1:13-14).

According to *The Pulpit Commentary,* the word rigor is a very rare one. It is derived from a root which means, *"to break in pieces, to crush."*

The tide had now turned completely. From the time that the children of Israel were looked at as favored guests because they were the relatives of Joseph, they now were hated, feared, and were actually made into slaves.

If the labor in the field included, as Josephus supposed, the cutting of canals, their lives would indeed have been made bitter. There is no toil as exhausting as that of working under the hot Egyptian sun from sunrise to sunset, with the feet in water, in an open cutting, where there can be no shade and scarcely a breath of air. This is what forced laborers are generally required to do. For instance, in the cutting of the Alexandrian Canal, 20,000 laborers out of 150,000 died as a result of the harsh conditions.

In such a social climate, at this stage, one would not have given the children of Israel any chance at all. They were servile slaves, and Egypt was the mightiest nation on earth, so what could they do?

THREE THINGS THAT WE
MUST TAKE INTO ACCOUNT

1. Irrespective of the plans that the evil Pharaoh would make, and regardless of what he thought, he would not have the final say, with that belonging to God.

2. These people belonged to God and not to Pharaoh. The evil monarch surely thought they belonged to him, but they didn't. As well, it should be remembered presently that every single believer in the world belongs to the Lord Jesus Christ. Irrespective as to where they might live, how totalitarian their government might be, or how bad the situation looks on the surface, these believers belong to God, and whatever is done to them is done unto God. That should be remembered!

3. Whatever God wants to do with His people, that He will do, and nothing will stop Him. If men get in the way, even the mightiest on the face of the earth

as Pharaoh, they will be subdued, while the slaves gain supremacy.

Pharaoh would have been 10,000 times better off had he treated these people with dignity and kindness. He would have spared the near destruction of his nation.

Then again, had Pharaoh made the lives of the children of Israel easy and profitable, the truth is, they would not have wanted to leave Egypt. So, the Lord makes even the wrath of man to praise Him (Ps. 76:10).

KING OF EGYPT

"And the king of Egypt spoke to the Hebrew midwives, of which the name of the one was Shiphrah, and the name of the other Puah" (Ex. 1:15).

Verses 15 through 22 portray the two leading Hebrew midwives, Shiphrah and Puah. It is ironic that the names of the mighty Pharaohs of that day are all but lost to history, whereas the names of these two women who obeyed God are recognized by multiple millions in every generation.

The faith of these brave women (for they risked their own lives) is recognized by God, and He dealt well with them. It must not be assumed that they were guilty of falsehood. There is no reason to suppose that what they stated was not perfectly true.

The statement in Verse 21, coupled with the statements of the prior verses, means that God protected these midwives from being put to death by Pharaoh, and that because of their faith, He made them houses, that is, He gave them large families.

The two named here were evidently in charge of many, if not all, of the midwives among the people of Israel.

To portray the eternal consequences of those who serve the Lord, as stated, this is so important that I want to say it again.

The Pharaoh of that particular time is not surely known at present, while the names of these two women, whomever they may have been, are known to millions and, in fact, have been known by millions in every generation.

This tells us that all that is merely human, however solid, brilliant, or attractive, must ultimately fall into the cold grasp of death and there molder in the dark, silent tomb. The clod of the valley must cover man's highest excellencies and brightest glories. Mortality is engraved upon his brow, and all his schemes are transitory.

On the contrary, that which is connected with and based upon God shall endure forever. Mackintosh said, *"His name shall endure forever, and His memorial to all generations."*

MIDWIVES

"And he said, When you do the office of a midwife to the Hebrew women, and see them upon the stools; if it be a son, then you shall kill him: but if it be a daughter, then she shall live.

"But the midwives feared God, and did not as the king of Egypt commanded them, but saved the men children alive.

"And the king of Egypt called for the midwives, and said unto them, Why have you done this thing, and have saved the men children alive?

"And the midwives said unto Pharaoh, Because the Hebrew women are not as the Egyptian women; for they are lively, and are delivered ere the midwives come in unto them.

"Therefore God dealt well with the midwives: and the people multiplied, and waxed very mighty.

"And it came to pass, because the midwives feared God, that He made them houses.

"And Pharaoh charged all his people, saying, Every son that is born you shall cast into the river, and every daughter you shall save alive" (Ex. 1:16-22).

These two women, Shiphrah and Puah, were in charge of all the midwives, who, no doubt, numbered into the thousands. Evidently, Shiphrah and Puah were called before Pharaoh, or at least one of his emissaries, and given instructions, which they were to give to all the midwives. Every boy baby was to be killed as soon as it was born, with only the little girl babies left alive. This murderous scheme hatched up by Pharaoh or someone in his court was supposed to weaken Israel by denying it further growth. As stated, they were multiplying mightily, with Pharaoh becoming more and more fearful of their size and power. Hence, they were reduced to abject slavery, and now this murderous scheme was concocted.

SOWING AND REAPING

Even though God uses all things, even the wrath of Pharaoh, still, what we sow, we must reap (Gal. 6:7). Whatever the actions of men in wickedness and high-handed rebellion, they are made subservient to the establishment of the divine counsels of grace and love. Even the wrath of man is yoked to the chariot wheel of God's decrees.

Why did God allow the descendants of Abraham to suffer such indignities and trials at the hands of the Egyptians?

As we have already briefly alluded, had Israel not suffered greatly, they certainly would not have wanted to leave Egypt. Also, Israel was not without blame. Great sin was in their camp, as well as in the camp of the Egyptians.

Going some 1,600 years into the future, Israel delivered up Christ into the hands of the Gentiles, and so into their hands, they also have been delivered. Christ was shamefully treated by the Romans, but yet, the same people were employed by God to punish the Jews. Christ was *"cut off"* out of the land of the living, and from A.D. 70, Israel, too, was cut off from the land of their fathers until 1948. Thus, we see again and again how inexorable is the outworking of the law of sowing and reaping.

As it regards Israel and Egypt, in a sense, Israel was paying for what they had done in the past. Remember the terrible sin against Joseph!

THE REAPING OF JUDGMENT CAN BE STOPPED!

In fact, it can only be stopped in one way, and that is by one's acceptance of Christ, which immediately stops all judgment of every description. Christ took all the judgment at the Cross. For God to continue to visit judgment upon a person who has truly come to Christ would be a mockery. It would, in essence, say that Christ did not finish His work, in other words, He did not take all of our judgment. However, He did take all of our judgment, and did so in totality.

Terrible things are sowed by all unbelievers, and to be sure, they will reap the result of what they have sowed as long as they remain in the unsaved state. However, the moment they come to Christ, the reaping of evil stops. While there might be a residue that carries over, even that can be greatly ameliorated.

THE FAMILY CURSE

There is a teaching presently referred to as *"the family curse,"* which has become very prominent and has confused many people. Let's look at that particular teaching:

Is there such a thing as a family curse?

Most definitely, there is such a thing as a family curse, a generational curse, and the curse of the broken law. In fact, every type of curse possibly that one could think is visited upon the human race.

However, that pertains to the unsaved part of the human race. The moment the believing sinner comes to Christ, making Him Lord and Saviour, all curses are completely stopped. What does the Scripture say?

"Christ has redeemed us from the curse of the law, being made a curse for us: for it is written, Cursed is every one who hangs on a tree:

"That the blessing of Abraham might come on the Gentiles through Jesus Christ; that we might receive the promise of the Spirit through faith" (Gal. 3:13–14).

Jesus handled every curse at the Cross. None were excluded, which means that no believer should ever believe the untruth that he is having problems because of a family curse.

Knowing that many Christians do have problems, what then is the cause?

A FAILURE TO UNDERSTAND
THE CROSS OF CHRIST

Believers have problems of every nature, unnecessarily so I might quickly add, because they do not understand the Message of the Cross. They are told by preachers that their problem is a family curse, and they need hands laid on them by a preacher who understands this problem, and then their difficulties will be solved.

Unfortunately, whatever happens to them when hands are laid on them will not stop their problems, with them finding themselves experiencing the same difficulties as they had previously. Jesus said, *"You shall know the truth, and the truth shall make you free"* (Jn. 8:32).

While we definitely believe in the laying on of hands, problems of the nature of which we speak will not respond to such, but only to proper faith evidenced in Christ and what Christ has done for us at the Cross.

All believers must understand that every single thing that comes to us from God comes exclusively by and through Christ and what Christ has done for us in His finished work. Consequently, we are to ever make the Cross the object of our faith, not allowing it to be moved to other things.

When we do this faithfully, which, in fact, is the very heart of the gospel, the Holy Spirit will then work mightily on our behalf, leading us into all truth and giving us victory over all things (Rom. 6:3-14; 8:1–11; Gal. 6:14; Col. 2:10–15).

THE CROSS ALONE IS THE ANSWER

That and that alone is the answer for the child of God. This means that the Cross holds the solution to every perplexing problem and the answer to every question. It is the means by which God gives all good things to His people.

So, how is it that certain preachers proclaim the family curse and other things as the problem?

They are deriving their teaching from an erroneous understanding of Exodus 20:5 and several other similar passages. That particular Scripture says: *"You shall not bow down yourself to them, nor serve them* (idols): *for I the*

LORD *your God am a jealous God, visiting the iniquity of the fathers upon the children unto the third and fourth generation of them who hate Me."*

The idea is that your great-great-grandfather, etc., did something terrible, and now you are reaping the results of that, hence, the family curse.

However, the Scripture mentions that it only comes upon those *"who hate Me,"* referring to the Lord. In fact, Verse 6 of Chapter 20 of Exodus says: *"And showing mercy unto thousands of them who love Me, and keep My commandments."*

While there is definitely such a thing as a family curse, and it definitely does come down to the third and fourth generations, it is only against those who hate the Lord. The moment that a person comes to Christ, the *"iniquity of the fathers"* is immediately suspended. The mercy of God takes over, which is a part of the born-again experience. That's the reason that Paul said:

"Therefore if any man be in Christ, he is a new creation: old things are passed away; behold, all things are become new" (II Cor. 5:17). Now, either the old things have passed away, or else, the Apostle Paul didn't tell the truth, and those things are still with us. I choose to believe that he told the truth.

Regrettably, and I think I am correct in my assumption, at that particular time, most among the children of Israel were not saved. They were not abiding by the covenant. While some certainly were, that number would have been few. I think all of this is proven by the difficulties which Moses experienced with them when the time finally came for them to be delivered. So, in a sense, the judgment of God was upon the Israelites and, a little later, would greatly come upon the Egyptians.

Let us say it again: All sin must be addressed and punished. It can either be punished by the judgment of God and the person ultimately dying eternally lost and going to hell, or else, the believing sinner can accept Christ, who has taken our punishment and suffered for us. Those are the two choices!

THE DESIGN OF SATAN

While Pharaoh desired to weaken the Israelites by demanding that the boy babies be killed at birth, Satan's plan was far more sinister. This is the serpent's enmity against the seed of the woman. Concerning the male children being destroyed, if this could have been carried out, there would have been no David, just to name one instance, and if no David, no David's Son.

Even though the midwives, no doubt, feared Pharaoh, they feared God more; consequently, they did not obey this wicked king.

All believers are to obey government unless such government violates our conscience and the Word of God. Then we must disobey but, at the same time, be prepared to pay the consequences. However, God would protect Shiphrah and Puah, and all others who assisted. Not only would the Lord protect them, but He would bless them, as well, by giving them large families, i.e., houses.

Not able to have his command obeyed as it regarded the little boy babies being killed at birth, Pharaoh demanded then that all boy babies be thrown into the river, with the girl babies alone being saved alive. As we shall see, the Lord greatly and wondrously used this to bring about His divine will also.

"Let us sing of His love once again.
"Of the love that can never decay,
"Of the blood of the Lamb who was slain.
"Till we praise Him again in that day."

"There are cleansing and healing for all
"Who will wash in the life-giving flood
"There is a life everlasting and joy
"At the right hand of God through the blood."

"Even now while we taste of His love
"We are filled with delight at His name;
"But when will it be when above
"We shall join in the song of the Lamb."

CHAPTER TWO

The Birth Of Moses

THE BIRTH OF MOSES

"And there went a man of the house of Levi, and took to wife a daughter of Levi" (Ex. 2:1).

Moses was a member of the tribe of Levi. He was the seventh from Abraham. Abraham was the seventh from Heber, and Enoch the seventh from Adam. Miriam and Aaron were already born when Moses was born. Jochebed was his mother, with Amram being his father.

Concerning the birth of Moses, *Ellicott's Commentary* said: *"Note the extreme simplicity of this announcement, and compare it with the elaborate legends wherewith Oriental religions commonly surrounded the birth of those who were considered their founders, as Thoth, Zoroaster, Orpheus. Even the name of the father is here omitted as unimportant. It is difficult to conceive anyone but Moses making such an omission."*

The phrase, *"daughter of Levi,"* doesn't mean that Jochebed was actually the daughter of Levi, who, in fact, had been dead many years, but rather that she was of the tribe of Levi.

COMMENTS

Concerning Moses, Arthur Pink said: *"From Adam to Christ there is none greater than Moses. He is one of the few characters of Scripture whose course is sketched from his infancy to his death. The fierce light of criticism has been turned upon him for generations, but he is still the most commanding figure of the ancient world.*

"In character, in faith, in the unique position assigned him as the mediator of the old covenant, and in achievements, he stands first among the heroes of the Old Testament.

"All of God's early dealings with Israel were transacted through Moses. He was a prophet, priest, and king in one person, and so united all the great and important functions which later were distributed among a plurality of persons. The history of such an one is worthy of the strictest attention, and his remarkable life deserves the closest study."

MORE COMMENTS

I. M. Haldeman said of this man Moses: *"The life of Moses presents a series of striking antithesis. For instance, he was the child of a slave, and the son of a queen. He was born in a hut, and lived in a palace. He inherited poverty, and enjoyed unlimited wealth. He was the leader of armies, and the keeper of flocks. He was the mightiest of warriors, and the meekest of men. He was educated in the court of Egypt, and yet dwelt in the desert. He had the wisdom of*

Egypt, and the faith of a child. He was fitted for the city, and wandered in the wilderness. He was tempted with the pleasures of sin, and endured the hardships of virtue. He was backward in speech, and yet talked with God. He had the rod of a shepherd, and the power of the Infinite. He was a fugitive from Pharaoh, and an ambassador from heaven. He was the giver of the law, and the forerunner of grace.

"He died alone on Mount Moab, and appeared with Christ in Judea. No man assisted at his funeral, yet God buried him."

THE FAITH OF JOCHEBED

"And the woman conceived, and bear a son: and when she saw him that he was a goodly child, she hid him three months.

"And when she could not longer hide him, she took for him an ark of bulrushes, and daubed it with slime and with pitch, and put the child therein; and she laid it in the flags by the river's brink.

"And his sister stood afar off, to wit what would be done to him" (Ex. 2:2-4).

That which stands out so vividly in this account is the faith of Jochebed, the mother of Moses.

I have no doubt that the Lord moved upon Jochebed from the time of the conception of Moses in her womb, in that she sensed that there was more here than met the eye. I believe that feeling not only persisted, but grew in intensity unto the time of her delivery. As well, when the child was born, she knew beyond the shadow of a doubt that there was something extensively unique about this baby; hence, she would go to any length to save its life.

Not being successful in attempting to force the mid-wives to kill the boy babies when they were born, Pharaoh issued another edict, which demanded that all boy babies be drowned in the Nile River at the time of their birth.

As we follow the narrative throughout the Scriptures, we see that Satan does everything within his power to kill those who are truly called of God. Concerning Christ and Satan, the Scripture says: *"Forasmuch then as the children are partakers of flesh and blood, He* (Christ) *also Himself likewise took part of the same* (became flesh and blood)*; that through death* (the crucifixion) *He might destroy him who had the power of death, that is, the Devil"* (Heb. 2:14).

The death which Pharaoh demanded was typical of the eternal death which Satan brought upon the human race as a result of the fall.

THE POWER OF DEATH

What did Paul mean by the term, *"the power of death,"* and that the Devil had this power?

Satan's power lies in the realm of sin. The Scripture says, *"the wages of sin is death"* (Rom. 6:23). Sin gives Satan the legal right to hold men in captivity, which leads to spiritual death and ultimately means eternal separation from God. In fact, the power of sin and death is so strong that before the

Cross, every saint of God who died, which included all of the Old Testament saints, did not go to heaven, but rather their souls and spirits were taken down into paradise in the heart of the earth and actually held captive there by Satan. While they were not over in the burning side of hell, with a great gulf separating the paradise side from the burning side (Lk. 16:26), still, they were held captive by the Evil One.

In other words, the sin debt still hung over them simply because the blood of bulls and goats could not take away sin. The sacrificial system was all that existed before the Cross and was a stopgap measure, if you will, until Christ would come (Heb. 10:4).

THE DEATH OF CHRIST

All the Old Testament saints were waiting for Christ, who had been promised, to become a partaker of flesh and blood, and we refer to the incarnation. His perfect human body would be offered up in sacrifice on the Cross, which would atone for all sin. When this happened, and it most definitely did happen, Jesus Christ then went down into paradise, and the Scripture says, *"He led captivity captive, and gave gifts unto men"* (Eph. 4:8).

The term, *He led captivity captive*, is a strange term, but yet, it holds a wealth of meaning. The word *captivity* refers to all the Old Testament saints held in captivity by Satan, even though he could not put them into the burning side of hell. However, when Jesus died on the Cross, He then went down into paradise and liberated every single one of these individuals. He, thereby, made them His captives and took them with Him to heaven. This was all because of the Cross, the price paid there, and all sin being atoned. Now, when a believer dies, and we speak of all time since the Cross, the saint immediately goes to heaven to be with Christ because there is no more sin debt hanging over the head of any child of God (Phil. 1:23).

Through death, which refers to the crucifixion, Jesus destroyed Satan's power of death because all sin was atoned. While the wages of sin still is death, because of what Jesus did at the Cross, any person who comes to Christ and expresses faith in Him can have every single sin washed away, which thereby destroys the power of death.

THROUGH DEATH

If it is to be noticed, it was through death that Jesus accomplished this, and not the resurrection, or by going down into the burning side of hell and suffering there as a sinner, as some teach such foolishness! It was through death that Christ accomplished this great thing, which refers to the Cross, and the Cross alone.

So, the death that Pharaoh proposed was actually Satan's motif; however, through this proposed death, the Lord would turn Pharaoh's edict into victory.

Jochebed hid baby Moses for three months. Incidentally, his name at the time was not Moses. We have no idea as to the name that Jochebed gave him, if any, because the name

Moses was actually given to him by the Egyptian princess who adopted him.

Led by the Holy Spirit and evidencing faith in God, and great faith at that, Jochebed made a little ark for baby Moses. She laid him in the ark, pushed it out into the Nile, and told his sister Miriam to watch from a distance to see what happened. I think that Jochebed had at least an inkling of knowledge as to what the Lord was going to do. I doubt that she understood it completely, but I believe the Lord told her exactly where to put the ark into the water, which was where the daughter of Pharaoh came to wash herself daily.

THE DAUGHTER OF PHARAOH

"And the daughter of Pharaoh came down to wash herself at the river; and her maidens walked along by the river's side; and when she saw the ark among the flags, she sent her maid to fetch it" (Ex. 2:5).

God is even in little things. He overrules the little things as well as the great things to help forward His purposes.

Little did this Egyptian princess think that day, as she walked by the river, that the God of the heavens (not the god that she worshipped) was directing her footsteps.

As someone has well said, *"God floated His navies on the tears on a baby's cheek."*

The Holy Spirit worked all of this out, even down to the minute details. He told Jochebed exactly what to do and had something in mind that Jochebed could not have possibly dreamed.

As previously stated, God works in little things as well as He does in the great things. In fact, He takes little things, such as this before us, and turns them into great things. However, all that God does is by and large done according to the faith of an individual. God seldom works beyond or without our faith. Jochebed had faith. She heard the voice of the Lord, and she obeyed the voice of the Lord. All of this required faith.

The Holy Spirit had everything timed just right — the place, the person, and the progress. The little ark was floating among the flags where the princess would bathe, and her eyes fell upon this which would prove to be such a major part in the great kingdom of God — Moses.

TEARS

"And when she had opened it, she saw the child: and, behold, the babe wept. And she had compassion on him, and said, This is one of the Hebrews' children" (Ex. 2:6).

The great power of God that particular day, at least in this instance, was brought down to the tears on a baby's cheeks.

Concerning this moment, George Williams writes: *"Great events have hung upon a tear, but never greater than those which were brought to pass by the tears of this baby! The defeat of Satan, the salvation of Israel and of the nations, the trustworthiness of God's Word, and the salvation of the world through an incarnate Saviour — all these lay hidden in the tears that wetted that infant cheek upon that day."*

FAITH

Let's once again look at faith as it regards the entirety of these actions, and especially that of Jochebed and her husband, Amram.

Though faith vanquished fear as it regards this couple, yet lawful means were used to overcome danger: The mother hid the child, and later, had recourse to the ark. It is not faith but fanaticism which deliberately courts danger. Faith never tempts God. Even Christ, though He knew full well of the Father's will to preserve Him, yet withdrew from those who sought His life (Lk. 4:30; Jn. 8:59). It is not lack of faith to avoid danger by legitimate precautions. It is no want of trust to employ means, even when assured by God of the event (Acts 27:31). Christ never supplied by a miracle when ordinary means were at hand (Mk. 5:43).

CIVIL AUTHORITIES

Another important truth, which here receives illustration and exemplification, is that civil authorities are to be defied when their decrees are contrary to the expressed Word of God. The Word of God requires us to obey the laws of the land in which we live and exhorts us to be subject unto the powers that be (Rom., Chpt. 13). This is true no matter how wise and just or how foolish and unjust those laws appear to us.

Yet, our obedience and submission to human authorities is plainly qualified. If a human government enacts a law and compliance with it by a saint would compel him to disobey some command or precept of God, then the human must be rejected for the divine. The cases of Moses' parents, of Daniel (Dan. 6:7-11), and of the apostles (Acts 5:29) establish this unequivocally. However, if such rejection of human authority be necessitated, let it be performed not in the spirit of carnal defiance, but in the fear of God, and then the issue may safely be left with Him. It was *by faith* the parents of Moses *"were not afraid of the king's commandment"* (Heb. 11:23). May divine grace work in us like precious faith, which overcomes all fear of man.

However, in disobeying laws which offend our conscience, and which are directly opposed to the Word of God, we must at first realize that there will be consequences, and that we have to be ready to face those consequences.

(The author is indebted to Arthur W. Pink for statements under the subheadings of Faith and Civil Authorities.)

A NURSE

"Then said his sister to Pharaoh's daughter, Shall I go and call to you a nurse of the Hebrew women, that she may nurse the child for you?

"And Pharaoh's daughter said to her, Go. And the maid went and called the child's mother.

"And Pharaoh's daughter said unto her, Take this child away, and nurse it for me, and I will give you your wages. And the woman took the child, and nursed it" (Ex. 2:7-9).

Evidently the baby was beautiful because immediately, the daughter of Pharaoh fell in love with the little fellow. Of course, we know the Lord had something to do with this as well.

About the time that Pharaoh's daughter picked up the child, for she no doubt did so, Moses' sister Miriam, who had been standing nearby, asked those there if she could get one of the Hebrew women to nurse the child. Miriam, as well, was led by the Lord in this.

Pharaoh's daughter instantly agreed that this would be the thing to do and told Miriam, with whom she was not acquainted, to go find a nurse. Guess what! Miriam went straight to her mother, who, as well, was the mother of the child. She immediately came to the river bank.

JOCHEBED

Pharaoh's daughter told her to take the child and care for it, and she would pay her wages to do so. Of course, she never dreamed that the lady to whom she gave the child was actually the child's mother.

So, Jochebed would take care of baby Moses and be paid by the state for doing so. I wonder what Satan thought of this! His plans to defeat the great plan of God were foiled, with the Lord even playing a little trick on the Evil One. Getting the court of Pharaoh, which had given instructions for the boy babies to be killed, to rather pay Jochebed to care for the child presents itself not only as a defeat for Satan, but also, an insult to the Evil One. I think from this, we have to come to the conclusion that God also has a sense of humor.

Can you imagine what Satan said to the demon spirits who were supposed to have been attending the funeral of little Moses!

THE ARK

Though Moses was brought to the place of death, he was made secure in the ark. This speaks to us of Christ, who went down into death for us. The righteousness of God made imperative the payment of sin's awful wages, and so his spotless Son died, *"the just for the unjust, that He might bring us to God"* (I Pet. 3:18).

It was faith that placed baby Moses in the ark, and it is faith that identifies us with Christ. Again, just as Moses was brought out of the place of death, so when Christ rose again, we rose with Him (Rom. 6:3–5; Eph. 2:5–6).

As well, as the heavenly Father arranged for the tender care of the baby, He also arranges the same care for us.

All that took place that day were in no way chance happenings. All were designed by the Holy Spirit, as all are always designed by the Holy Spirit, at least as it regards those who follow the Lord.

From this, we can take a lesson as to how minutely the Lord leads and guides and how He plans every detail, and under grace, we can be certain that His protection and care are certainly no less.

MOSES

"And the child grew, and she brought him unto Pharaoh's daughter, and he became her son. And she called his name Moses: and she said, Because I drew him out of the water" (Ex. 2:10).

To show how little the Holy Spirit thought of the palace of Pharaoh, He, in effect, devoted one verse to those years of Moses' life.

There are two passages in the New Testament which throw a little light on Verse 10. In Acts 7:22, we read: *"and Moses was learned in all the wisdom of the Egyptians, and was mighty in words and in deeds."*

Josephus gave the following as it regarded this particular time of Moses' life. He told us that the daughter of Pharaoh was named Thermuthis and that she was married but childless.

Josephus went on to say that when Moses was weaned, which was probably at 4 or 5 years old, Thermuthis then took him. At a point in time, she brought the child to her father and said, *"I am bringing up a beautiful, well-behaved child. Since I received him from the bounty of the river, I thought best to adopt him as my son and heir of your kingdom."* It is said that with that, she put the infant into his hands. Pharaoh took the child, kissed him, and playfully put his crown upon the little boy's head, but it is said that Moses threw it down to the ground and trod upon it with his feet in mere childishness.

EGYPT

However, as Josephus continued to relate, an Egyptian scribe was nearby and saw this. He had earlier prophesied and foretold that a child would be born to the Hebrews who would reduce the dominion of Egypt. Upon seeing the little boy Moses trod upon the crown, the scribe made a violent attempt to kill him. He cried out, *"This, O king, is that child we must kill to calm our terror! He shows it by treading upon your crown. Kill him and deliver us from our fear, and thus deprive the Hebrews of the hope he inspires!"*

However, Thermuthis stopped him by snatching the child away. Giving in to his daughter rather than the scribe, Pharaoh passed it off as a joke. Moses was, instead, educated with great care.

When grown to be a man, war broke out between the Egyptians and their neighbors, the Ethiopians. They fought a great battle, in which the Ethiopians were victorious, and they determined to conquer all of Egypt. Their armies invaded as far as Memphis and the sea.

Overtaken by this calamity, the Egyptians turned to oracles and divinations. During this time, someone mentioned Moses and his great ability, and they were urged to seek his assistance and even make him their general. So, Pharaoh commanded his daughter to produce him, which she did.

THE WISDOM OF MOSES

She made her father swear he would not harm him and then brought in Moses, but she reproached the priests who had previously advised to kill him and were now not ashamed to ask his help.

Moses went out, leading a great army, and he surprised the enemy before they knew he was coming. They expected that he would attack them by water since the interior was difficult to traverse due to the vast number of poisonous snakes that infested that area. However, Moses devised a marvelous strategy. So says Josephus.

Upon inquiring by Pharaoh and others as to how he planned to defeat the Ethiopians, it is said that Moses told them that he would take basketfuls of ibises, which are birds that devour serpents and are their greatest enemy. As soon as he would reach the infested region, he would release the birds, which would drive the serpents away. It is stated that Moses did this and then achieved his march and defeated the Ethiopians in a surprise attack. It is further stated that the Ethiopians fled Egypt and were pursued by Moses into their own country and defeated again, to the extent that they were in danger of being reduced to slavery.

There is no biblical proof of these happenings; however, it is quite possible that it happened as Josephus related.

There is another passage in Hebrews that throws more light on Verse 10, which we will address momentarily.

THE NAME MOSES

The Egyptian form of the name *Moses* was probably *Mesu*, which signifies *"born, brought forth, child,"* and is derived from a root meaning *"to produce, draw forth."* The Egyptian language has many roots common to it with Hebrew, whereof this is one.

The princess' play upon words thus admitted of being literally rendered in the Hebrew — *"She called his name Mosheh, which means, 'drawn forth'; because, she said, I drew him forth from the water."* Incidentally, the name *Mesu* is found on the monuments as an Egyptian name under the Nineteenth Dynasty. It could well be *Moses*.

THE FLESH

"And it came to pass in those days, when Moses was grown, that he went out unto his brethren, and looked on their burdens: and he spied an Egyptian smiting an Hebrew, one of his brethren.

"And he looked this way and that way, and when he saw that there was no man, he killed the Egyptian, and hid him in the sand.

"And when he went out the second day, behold, two men of the Hebrews strove together: and he said to him who did the wrong, Wherefore did you smite your fellow?" (Ex. 2:11-13).

From the language of Hebrews 11:24, it is clear that a time came when Moses had the choice of accepting or refusing the throne of Egypt. He refused and cast in his lot with the hated and oppressed Hebrews.

Moved by indignation, compassion, and a consciousness of personal fitness for the enterprise, he resolved to deliver them from their cruel bondage. However, God cannot give victories to the flesh, and Moses had to spend 40 long years as a shepherd in the deserts of Arabia in order to fit him to be a shepherd to Israel.

An important principle appears in this chapter. It is that providence and faith must not be confounded. Providence gave Moses (the palace) what faith taught him to surrender.

Earthly wisdom counseled him to use his position in the Egyptian court as a means for liberating his people. This would have spared him much affliction, but it would have recognized Pharaoh's lordship, and would have wholly failed to separate Israel from Egypt and bring her into fellowship with, and dependence upon, God.

THE FLESH CANNOT DO
WHAT ONLY GOD CAN DO

Moses had now come to the place to where he must make a decision. The result of his faith is described in Hebrews 11:24-26: *"By faith Moses, when he was come to years, refused to be called the son of Pharaoh's daughter; choosing rather to suf-*

fer affliction with the people of God, than to enjoy the plea-
sures of sin for a season; esteeming the reproach of Christ
greater riches than the treasures in Egypt: for he had respect
unto the recompense of the reward."

Josephus further told us that Pharaoh had no other children and that his daughter, Thermuthis, had no children of her own. So, most probably, Moses would have succeeded to the throne.

Were this scene transported to the present day, I can well imagine what the counsel would be to Moses as it regards the modern church.

Most, I am certain, would definitely tell Moses that he could do far more for God by remaining in the palace of Pharaoh, and even becoming Pharaoh, than he could otherwise. The modern church sells out for far less, so I cannot see the modern church telling Moses to do what he actually did do. He refused to be called the son of Pharaoh's daughter, which means that he refused the throne of Egypt.

While God was dealing with him about all of this, still, it was Moses who had to ultimately make the decision as to what he would do.

The account of him killing the Egyptian who was smiting the Hebrew is not meant to claim that Moses, at that time, was trying to deliver his people. He was merely trying to address an injustice; however, he was trying to do it in the wrong way, i.e., the flesh.

Then again, the Lord could well have been dealing with Moses about this task, although it would be many years before Moses was ready.

WHAT DO WE MEAN BY "THE FLESH?"

Paul used the term very often. He said, *"So then they who are in the flesh cannot please God"* (Rom. 8:8).

The flesh pertains to our own personal strength, ability, talent, efforts, will power, motivation, education, etc. Paul described that as walking after the flesh (Rom. 8:1). The capabilities of man to live for God by his own personal strength were forever thwarted by the fall in the garden of Eden. This left man so incapacitated in every capacity that it made it impossible for him to do what needs to be done.

So, God's solution to this dilemma is *"Jesus Christ and Him crucified."* While the Holy Spirit works exclusively within the parameters of the finished work of Christ, and He will not work outside of those boundaries, this means that our faith must not be in ourselves, not at all, but rather in Christ and what He did for us at the Cross. Then the Holy Spirit can do great and mighty things in our hearts and lives. Now, that is God's way. He only has one way simply because no other way is needed. It is the Cross! The Cross! The Cross!

WALKING AFTER THE SPIRIT

Most every person who is truly born again and Spirit-filled desires strongly to *"walk after the Spirit."* However, if these people were asked how that is to be done, most would draw a blank. If they did venture forth an answer, most of the time, it would be by applying more flesh instead of less.

After the believing sinner is saved, he must quickly come to the conclusion that what needs to be done, he cannot do. He must understand that God's way is the Cross of Christ. It was there that sin was finished once and for all (Heb. 7:27).

The believer must understand that the price was paid at Calvary's Cross, meaning that nothing is left owing. This means that Satan and all of his cohorts of darkness are defeated and that we as believers can walk in victory. While the Bible does not teach sinless perfection, it most definitely does teach that sin is not to have dominion over us (Rom. 6:14).

Let me say first of all: If the believer doesn't understand the Cross of Christ as it regards the sanctification of the saint — in other words, how we live for God, how we order our behavior, and how we gain victory over the world, the flesh, and the Devil — he simply cannot walk after the Spirit. It's just that simple!

So, what is walking after the Spirit?

When believers read Romans 8:1, we definitely do not want to walk after the flesh, but rather to walk after the Spirit. However, the trouble is, most believers, as stated, simply don't know how to do that. They think that doing spiritual things constitutes walking after the Spirit.

It doesn't!

It is impossible for any believer to walk after the Spirit without that believer properly understanding the Cross. The Holy Spirit works exclusively within the boundaries of the legal work of the Cross of Christ, in other words, what Jesus did at the Cross all on our behalf.

Listen again to Paul: *"For the law of the Spirit of life in Christ Jesus has made me free from the law of sin and death"* (Rom. 8:2).

In this one verse of Scripture, we are told how the Holy Spirit works.

All of this is so ironclad that it is referred to by the Spirit of God through Paul as a law. This refers to a law that was devised in eternity past by the Godhead. It is *"the law of the Spirit of life,"* which refers to all the things the Holy Spirit does.

THIS LAW

It goes back to the statement made by Christ at the Feast of Tabernacles. He said: *"If any man thirst, let him come unto Me, and drink.*

"He who believes on Me, as the Scripture has said, out of his belly shall flow rivers of living water."

John then added, *"But this spake He of the Spirit, which they who believe on Him should receive"* (Jn. 7:37–39).

The idea is this: all that Jesus paid for at the Cross is made available to us by and through the Holy Spirit, who demands that our faith be in Christ and what He did for us at the Cross.

However, this law is *"in Christ Jesus,"* which means that it is all based on what Christ did for us in His finished work. This means that the Holy Spirit will not work outside of these boundaries. The drawn parameters are those which incorporate what Christ did at the Cross regarding His finished work. The Cross gives the Holy Spirit the legal right to do all the things He does.

That's the reason that we must exhibit faith in Christ and the Cross at all times. In fact, the following will help you. It is a short formula that possibly may make it easier to understand.

JESUS CHRIST

We must understand that everything we receive from God, and I mean everything, all and without exception is made possible by the Lord Jesus Christ. He alone is the source (Jn. 1:1-3, 14, 17, 29).

THE CROSS OF CHRIST

The Cross is the means by which all of these wonderful things are done for us. In other words, it's the Cross which made it all possible. When we speak of the Cross, we aren't speaking of the wooden beam on which Jesus died, but rather what He there accomplished (Rom. 6:1-14; Col. 2:10-15).

THE OBJECT OF FAITH

With our Lord as the source and the Cross as the means, the object of our faith must ever be Christ and the Cross. In fact, the entirety of the story of the Bible is *"Jesus Christ and Him crucified"* (I Cor. 1:23; 2:2).

THE HOLY SPIRIT

With our Lord as the source and the Cross as the means, and Christ and the Cross as the object of our faith, the Holy Spirit, who works exclusively within the parameters of the finished work of Christ, will work mightily on our behalf (Rom. 8:1-11; Eph. 2:13-18). In fact, most believers do not have the slightest clue as to how the Holy Spirit works. They are acquainted with some things that He does, but almost no acquaintance whatsoever with the manner in which He works in order to give us the power that we need. It is all tied to the Cross of Christ.

PHARAOH AND MOSES

"And he said, Who made you a prince and a judge over us? do you intend to kill me, as you killed the Egyptian? And Moses feared, and said, Surely this thing is known.

"Now when Pharaoh heard this thing, he sought to kill Moses. But Moses fled from the face of Pharaoh, and dwelt in the land of Midian: and he sat down by a well" (Ex. 2:14-15).

Quoting Josephus again, it seems that from the throne down, the Egyptians were envious of Moses and partly afraid of him. Due to his great success in defeating the Ethiopians, they thought that he might take advantage of his good fortune and try to subvert their government. So, when Moses, in defending the Hebrew, killed an Egyptian, this was the proverbial straw that broke the camel's back. Pharaoh then prepared to kill Moses. Learning that there were plots against him, Moses secretly escaped across the desert since the roads were patrolled.

The next day after killing the Egyptian, he saw two Hebrews fighting among themselves and proceeded to stop the scuffle. One of the Hebrews said to him, *"Who made you a prince and a judge over us? do you intend to kill me, as you killed the Egyptian?"*

Realizing that his secret was out, Moses fled Egypt, and not a minute too soon. If Moses had any thoughts of delivering the children of Israel at this particular time, to be sure, they were now placed on the back burner. He was fleeing for his life.

At any rate, it was not God's time at the present, and for several reasons. Moses wasn't ready, not even close to being ready, and neither were the Israelites ready to be delivered.

MOSES IN THE PALACE

There are some, actually many, who claim that the some 35 years that Moses spent in the palace (probably taken to the palace when he was about 5 years old) was a part of his education, which would greatly help him in delivering Israel some 40 years after leaving the palace.

We do know that it was God's will that Moses spend this amount of time there, but I seriously doubt that all the education he received from the Egyptians did him any stead whatsoever, as it regarded the work for which God had called him to do. Everything that Moses did in delivering these people, even their 40-year trek through the wilderness, was all designed by God down to the minute detail. I speak of organization, supply, discipline, etc. In fact, there is no record that Moses ever used any of his Egyptian education in this endeavor. So, if, in fact, that is the case, what purpose was the long stay in the palace and all the educational process?

GREAT FAITH MUST BE TESTED GREATLY

For the task that lay ahead for Moses, at least that which God had called him to do, total and complete consecration would be required. As someone has well said, *"Great faith must be tested greatly."*

I can well see that the Lord would have Moses go through these many years of education and training in order to test him as to his consecration. This would especially include the throne of Egypt being his for the taking, which, in effect, would make him at least one of, if not the most, powerful man in the world. We know what his decision was: *"By faith Moses, when he was come to years, refused to be called the son of Pharaoh's daughter"* (Heb. 11:24). So, we know that Moses had to make this decision.

Considering the task that Moses had before him, it would take an unparalleled consecration, with him completely and totally turning his back on the world, even the best the world had to offer. The Lord had to have that type of consecration. So, that's the reason, I think, that the Lord allowed all of those years in the palace of Pharaoh and even the offer of the throne.

MIDIAN

"Now the priest of Midian had seven daughters: and they came and drew water, and filled the troughs to water their father's flock.

"And the shepherds came and drove them away: but Moses stood up and helped them, and watered their flock.

"And when they came to Reuel their father, he said, How is it that you are come so soon today?

"And they said, An Egyptian delivered us out of the hand of the shepherds, and also drew water enough for us, and watered the flock.

"And he said unto his daughters, And where is he? why is it that you have left the man? call him, that he may eat bread.

"And Moses was content to dwell with the man: and he gave Moses Zipporah his daughter.

"And she bare him a son, and he called his name Gershom: for he said, I have been a stranger in a strange land" (Ex. 2:16-22).

Moses, like Joseph, was rejected by his brethren; and, like Joseph, he continued to love them.

The priest of Midian had three names: Reuel, Jethro, and Raguel. This latter name means, "a friend of God." He was a descendant of Abraham by Keturah. He, no doubt, like Job and Melchizedek, was king and priest to his tribe. He was a worshipper of the true God.

Moses was about to begin his true education of 40 years' duration. Some have said that it took about 40 hours to get Moses out of Egypt but about 40 years to get Egypt out of Moses.

REDUCED TO POVERTY

For most of his boyhood and all of his adult life, Moses had enjoyed the luxury, splendor, grandeur, and greatness of the Egyptian court, but now, he was reduced to penury, for it seems that he left Egypt with nothing.

Moses is a type of Christ in many ways. As Moses came from grandeur to nothing, so did Christ. He left the hallowed halls of heaven to come down here to this sin-benighted world.

We must assume that the Lord led Moses to Jethro (Reuel) and that Zipporah was destined to be his wife. But yet, Zipporah didn't prove to be as close to Moses as she should have been. There were serious problems there, which would later show up. In fact, the future would show that his son did not turn out too well either, possibly because of the influence of the boy's mother.

How much grief this caused Moses, we have no way of knowing; however, it is for certain that these situations were not taken lightly, especially considering the heavy load which he had to carry regarding the call of God on his life.

How blessed a man is, especially a preacher, to have a godly wife, who will stand with him shoulder to shoulder, with both pulling together to carry out the great work of God. However, Moses didn't really have that.

THE CRY OF THE CHILDREN OF ISRAEL

"And it came to pass in process of time, that the king of Egypt died: and the children of Israel sighed by reason of the bondage, and they cried, and their cry came up unto God by reason of the bondage" (Ex. 2:23).

The pressure from Egypt was now becoming so hard and so difficult on the Israelites that they were now ready to leave. To be frank, they would in no way have left Egypt had the blessings continued as it was during the time of Joseph. At times, the Lord has to allow difficulties in order for us to become willing to do His will.

It was now time for the covenant that God had made with Abraham, Isaac, and Jacob, regarding the land of Canaan, to be fulfilled. God always keeps His promises.

God looked upon the children of Israel exactly as He looks upon all believers.

The glorious name *Elohim* occurs five times in Verses 23 through 25. As yet, He was not known to Israel as Jehovah. Five is the number of grace. No moral excellence in the children of Israel attracted God's love; it was their misery that drew out His heart to them:

- He *heard* their groaning.
- He *remembered* His covenant.
- He *looked* upon them.
- He had *respect* unto them.

Moses had now been in Midian, actually the backside of the desert, for some 40 years. Except for the last days in this place, which gives us the account of the burning bush, the Scriptures are silent regarding this time.

GOD HEARD THE CRY OF THE CHILDREN OF ISRAEL

Verses 23 through 25 portray the misery and bondage of the children of Israel. It is not clear here how much the Israelites were conscious of God or whether they had almost forgotten Him. We do know that it was God who took the initiative in their deliverance in view of His covenants and promises to their fathers.

As well, it is God who takes the initiative in our salvation. Many people proclaim, *"I found the Lord,"* when, in reality, the Lord found us.

Perhaps a few in Israel knew God, but as a whole, the enslaved nation was in apostasy and rebellion. So, God did not deliver them on the face of their merit because they had none; He delivered them solely because of His grace, His love, and His promises. Likewise, God does not save us because we merit salvation, but He does so because He loves us and because He has promised redemption.

The Scripture says that the children of Israel were sighing by reason of the bondage, and as a result, they cried. However, it doesn't say that they were crying to God. They were just crying *"by reason of the bondage."*

God heard their cries exactly as He hears our cries. He is never unaware of our situation, irrespective as to what the situation might be. We are His children, bought with a price, the price, in fact, which was paid by Christ at the Cross of Calvary.

If He heard their cry, even though they were not necessarily crying to Him, how much more does He hear our cries when we truly cry to Him!

THE COVENANT

"And God heard their groaning, and God remembered His covenant with Abraham, with Isaac, and with Jacob.

"And God looked upon the children of Israel, and God had respect unto them" (Ex. 2:24-25).

As we've already stated, all of the initiative is on the part of God. There is no record that any of the children of Israel at this particular time truly and sincerely sought the face of the Lord concerning their particular situation. The faith that Jochebed and Amram evidenced seems to be little in evidence at this particular time. Forty years from their day unto the time in question had taken their deadly toll, spiritually speaking. While the Lord was remembered and not totally strange to them, there was very little faith. That's what it always comes down to, faith, or a lack of faith.

However, God had made a covenant with Abraham, Isaac, and Jacob. He had promised the land of Canaan to their seed, and God always keeps His promises. And yet, as it regards this particular generation, and I speak of the ones who came out of Egypt, only two of the adults actually went into the Promised Land. Those two were Joshua and Caleb, and it was because of their faith.

The children of Israel became so burdened down with oppression that they were ready to be delivered, but they were not ready to obey God in the wilderness. In fact, their lack of faith kept them out of the Promised Land.

As God looked upon the children of Israel in Egypt, He had respect unto them simply because they were the seed of Abraham, Isaac, and Jacob. In essence, the faith of these three would deliver this multitude, even though they had long since been dead. However, borrowed faith can go just so far. When initiative is needed, it must be the faith of the individual and not that borrowed from someone else. Regrettably, Israel lacked such faith, even as we shall see in later study.

> *"Alas, and did my Saviour bleed?*
> *"And did my Sovereign die?*
> *"Would He devote that sacred head*
> *"For such a worm as I?"*

"Was it for sins that I had done
"He groaned upon the tree?
"Amazing pity! Grace unknown!
"And love beyond degree!"

"Well might the sun in darkness hide,
"And shut his glories in,
"When Christ, the mighty Maker died
"For man, the creature's sin."

"Thus might I hide my shamed face
"While His dear Cross appears,
"Dissolve my heart in thankfulness,
"And melt my eyes to tears."

"But drops of grief can never repay
"The debt of love I owe:
"Here, Lord, I give myself to Thee;
" 'Tis all that I can do."

Moses And The Backside Of The Desert

MOSES AND THE BACKSIDE OF THE DESERT

"Now Moses kept the flock of Jethro his father in law, the priest of Midian: and he led the flock to the backside of the desert, and came to the mountain of God, even to Horeb" (Ex. 3:1).

The first verse tells us so very much about the ways of God. What God would do with Moses was not learned in the palaces of Egypt but was learned at *"the backside of the desert."*

Forty years of the desert was needed to humble the strength of the flesh and to destroy its hope. The possible king of Egypt was now an obscure shepherd.

The backside of the desert is not exactly where most people would aspire to be; however, it was here that the Lord appeared to Moses.

God not only gave to Moses the faith that led him to identify himself with His people, but also endowed him with the power to deliver them. However, 40 years in the desert was needed to humble the strength of the flesh and destroy its hope.

The latter, and we speak of deliverance, was far more difficult than the former, i.e., identification. It is the same presently.

Identification with Christ is not all that difficult. In fact, untold millions clamor to experience such identification; however, at first, they think it's an identification with His miracle-working power, His person of deity, or His great glory. That it is; however, for the hope of the flesh to be destroyed, we must, as well, identify with Him in His crucifixion, which alone can bring about deliverance. Now, read those words carefully because they are very, very important!

It cost Moses something to identify with His people, but much more to identify with their deliverance.

THE CROSS

That's why the Cross, with which we must identify, is such an offense (Gal. 5:11).

Why is the Cross of Christ an offense?

It is an offense because it demands total surrender to Christ and completely trusting in what Christ did at the Cross, all on our behalf. The Cross tells us how evil and wicked that man actually is and how wonderful and good that God actually is.

Man doesn't want to admit either! To admit that he is so bad that he cannot save himself rubs him the wrong way. To admit that God alone can save us and that He had to do such by the means of a Cross because we were so evil doesn't set well either.

Then, when preachers or believers come face-to-face with the exposure of the Cross, meaning that the Cross of Christ lays waste all of man's efforts, it shows them to be totally worthless. Man does not like that, and religious man does not like that most of all. Religious man is perfectly willing to put himself out, to extend himself, and to exhaust his own resources toward some certain religious goal because it ministers to his self-importance.

The Cross of Christ lays waste man's importance, and man doesn't like that. It offends him, therefore, the rejection of the Cross. At the same time, there is the insistence by God that man come by the means of the Cross, and only by the means of the Cross.

When Moses identified with Christ in preference to Egypt, for that's exactly what he did, as stated, there was a price tag attached to that. The Scripture says that he esteemed *"the reproach of Christ greater riches than the treasures in Egypt"* (Heb. 11:26). However, what he then experienced was nothing by comparison to what he experienced regarding preparation for deliverance. Even though his identification was proper, he had to be delivered himself before the children of Israel could experience deliverance by his hand.

This process was long, slow, hard, and tedious, and it was not that any of that earned him anything, but simply that the flesh dies hard. To be sure, it must totally and completely die before deliverance can come and, thereby, others be delivered as well.

DELIVERANCE FROM WHAT?

The deliverance, whether of Moses or any other believer, is always in one capacity, deliverance from the flesh. As we've stated, all hope of the flesh must die. Self is our biggest problem. As someone has well said, *"Jesus died on the Cross not only to save us from sin but, as well, from self."*

When we think of deliverance, almost always, we think of deliverance from particular vices, sins, etc. While that definitely may be the case and, in fact, may be necessary, that is never the center of real deliverance. It is the flesh from which we must be delivered, which refers to dependence on self. When that is done, and done completely, then the other problems will melt away.

How can that be done?

There's only one way, and that is by faith in Christ and what Christ has done for us at the Cross. It is to the Cross that we must come in order to be delivered from the work of the flesh. As well, it is at the Cross that we must remain after we're delivered from the work of the flesh.

By the term, *the mountain of God,* Sinai seems to be meant. The phrase, even to Horeb, should have been translated, *"even toward Horeb."*

MORE ABOUT THE BACKSIDE OF THE DESERT

This position in which Moses now found himself, and 40 years at that, was a position in which he was placed by the

Lord. The manner in which the Lord teaches us is totally different from the ways of the world. Self had to be humbled, and all hope of the flesh had to die.

I believe that Moses sensed the call of God on his life as it regarded the deliverance of the Israelites and the great part he would play in this process. How much the Lord had related to him up to now, we aren't told. Those 40 years are all but silent; however, as silent as they may have been, much was taking place. Moses was being prepared for the greatest task, at least up to that time, that any man had ever known. Due to interaction with Pharaoh and the nobles of Egypt, it was even more demanding than what God had asked of Noah.

One of the great problems with most modern preachers is they have had no *"backside of the desert"* experience. They've been trained by everyone and everything except God.

WHAT TYPE OF PREPARATION WAS REQUIRED?

Mere human wisdom and learning, however valuable within themselves, can never make anyone a servant of God or equip him for any department of divine service. Such things may qualify unrenewed nature to figure before the world, but the man whom God will use must be endowed with widely different qualifications — such qualifications as can alone be found in the deep and hallowed retirement of the Lord's presence.

All God's servants have been made to know and experience the truth of these statements. Moses at Horeb, Elijah at Cherith, Ezekiel at Chebar, Paul in Arabia, and John at Patmos are all striking examples of the immense practical importance of being alone with God. When we look at the Son of God, we find that the time He spent in private was nearly 10 times as long as that which He spent in public. Though perfect in understanding and in will, He spent nearly 30 years in the obscurity of a carpenter's house at Nazareth ere He made His appearance in public. Even when He had entered upon His public service, how often did He retreat from the gaze of men to enjoy the sweet and sacred retirement of the Divine Presence!

THE ABNEGATION OF SELF

The training that is required is the abnegation of self and the laying aside of the flesh. On the surface, that seems so simple, but in reality, it is not simple at all. It took 40 years for this thing to be brought about in Moses, more than 20 years for David, several years for Paul …

It was much more difficult in Old Testament times for this work of the Spirit to be brought about in these hearts and lives than it is now. The Cross has made it possible for the Holy Spirit to take up abode permanently within our hearts and lives, which gives all believers since the Cross a tremendous advantage. Still, it's not something that's done instantly.

Due to the fall, the lingering effects remain in the hearts and lives of even the most ardent believers. There is a strong inclination to promote self, in which climate Christ cannot work.

The only way that such victory can be brought about in any heart and life, whether Old Testament times or New Testament times, is for the believer to look exclusively to the Cross. It was much more difficult in Old Testament times because the Cross was a prophetic happening, in other words, something that would take place in the future. Inasmuch as that great work had not yet been accomplished, its effectiveness was extremely limited, as would be obvious. However, now that we look to a historical Cross, which speaks of a finished work, it is a much simpler process.

THE CROSS

A proper understanding of the Cross brings about humility within the heart and life, and, in fact, it is the Cross alone which can bring about this work of the Spirit. The believer is to ever make the Cross the object of his faith, and then the Holy Spirit can perform His work, which refers to dealing with the adverse situations in our hearts and lives. Once again, we're speaking of self and the flesh. In fact, without a proper understanding of the Cross, it is literally impossible for these particular works of the Spirit to be brought about. The Cross is God's way, and if we attempt some other way, we automatically abrogate the help of the Holy Spirit; consequently, nothing can really be accomplished in our lives.

However, irrespective of the hang-ups, idiosyncrasies, problems, difficulties, hindrances, weaknesses, perversions, or whatever other problem we might think of, the Holy Spirit can deal with that problem if our faith is properly placed, and I continue to speak of the Cross. At the Cross, Jesus addressed every single problem that besets humanity. He excluded none!

THE BURNING BUSH

"And the angel of the LORD appeared unto him in a flame of fire out of the midst of a bush: and he looked, and, behold, the bush burned with fire, and the bush was not consumed" (Ex. 3:2).

The *"angel of the LORD"* mentioned here is, in actuality, the Lord Himself.

The flame of fire in the lowly desert bush was an emblem of the deity and humanity of Christ. The fire pertained to the deity, and the lowly bush pertained to the humanity of Christ, but yet, the fire did not consume the bush.

As another issue, this is a perfect example of the Holy Spirit functioning in the heart and life of the believer. While the Spirit is doing what needs to be done, irrespective as to how hard it might be, there is no danger of the bush, i.e., you and me, being consumed. However, when we try to do the work by the strength of the flesh, we will soon experience burnout. So, how do we come to this place of the fire burning brightly but not consuming us?

WALKING AFTER THE SPIRIT

In Romans 8:1, Paul mentioned walking *"after the Spirit,"* which, of course, refers to the Holy Spirit. This simply means that the Spirit of God is leading and guiding us and, as well, functioning within us in order that the work of God may be properly carried out. Once again, we go back to the Cross.

Walking after the Spirit is not us doing something that we think is spiritual. No matter how spiritual it might be, whatever is happening in that capacity constitutes the flesh.

Let the reader understand this: It is never what we do, but rather what we believe. Of course, if we *believe* correctly, we will *do* correctly.

Listen to Paul: *"For in Jesus Christ neither circumcision availeth anything, nor uncircumcision; but faith which worketh by love"* (Gal. 5:6).

Then: *"But without faith it is impossible to please Him"* (Heb. 11:6).

Once more: *"Therefore being justified by faith ..."* (Rom. 5:1).

We keep trying to bring about things by doing because we are walking *"after the flesh"* (Rom. 8:1). We can only bring about the desired result by believing properly. This means that we must have the correct object of faith.

THE OBJECT OF OUR FAITH

Every human being in the world has faith. Unfortunately, it's not the type of faith that God will recognize, at least for the far greater majority; nevertheless, all have faith. Even the atheist who claims he doesn't have any faith, in fact, does, because he has faith in his lack of faith.

So, the question isn't faith. The question is, *"What is the correct object of faith?"*

There is only one correct object of faith, while there are untold thousands of incorrect objects. That one correct object is *"Christ and Him crucified"* (I Cor. 1:17–18, 21, 23; 2:2, 5; Col. 2:10–15; Gal. 5:1–2, 4; 6:14).

In this manner, and this manner alone, will the fire burn within our lives without consuming the bush.

BURNOUT

After Frances and I began in evangelistic work in 1956, for years I heard preachers speaking of burnout. Countless times, preachers would ask me if I had a hobby. This was supposed to be the answer to burnout.

No, that's no answer at all. It is the flesh attempting to throttle the flesh, which, of course, will never work. The answer is the Cross, and the answer alone is the Cross.

Serving in evangelistic work for many years and having the opportunity to be around many preachers, I witnessed many who experienced nervous breakdowns and emotional disturbances, in other words, burnout. It was then said of them that they had burned themselves out for Christ, meaning they had worked so hard for the Lord that they had overdone the situation, etc.

Inasmuch as this was many, many years ago, and most of the time, I was younger than the preachers in question, I never had any opinion on the subject. However, then I came to realize what faith really is, and above all, what the object of faith actually is, which gave me some insight into burnout.

No, that was not their problem. Their problem was functioning in the flesh, which means they were not functioning in the Spirit. How do I know that?

Were they functioning in the Spirit, no matter how brightly the fire burned, it would never consume the bush. In fact, it invigorates the man instead of tearing him down. It's our own efforts of the flesh that bring about emotional disturbances, problems, difficulties, etc. It's trying to do what we cannot do, and which God never intended for us to do because Jesus has already done it.

MOSES, MOSES

"And Moses said, I will now turn aside, and see this great sight, why the bush is not burnt.

"And when the LORD *saw that he turned aside to see, God called unto him out of the midst of the bush, and said, Moses, Moses. And he said, Here am I"* (Ex. 3:3-4).

God who said *"Moses, Moses,"* is the same One who said, *"Martha, Martha," "Simon, Simon," "Saul, Saul,"* and also, *"Samuel, Samuel."* It was the same voice that said, *"I have surely seen," "I have heard," "I know," "I am come down to deliver,"* and *"I am come to bring up."*

In a sense, everything that God does is in the form of a miracle. That's the reason faith is required, and that's the reason, or at least one of the reasons, that self and the flesh have to be abrogated, or rather properly placed in Christ.

As we see here, God does not function as does anything else. His ways are not our ways, and it takes faith to comprehend His ways. So, now Moses would turn aside to see the bush that was burning, but yet, was not consumed. Now, out of the midst of the bush, God would speak to the man.

Nothing can be more interesting or instructive than the mode in which Jehovah was pleased to reveal Himself to Moses. He was about to furnish him with his commission to lead forth His people out of Egypt. As well, He would reveal Himself as a flame of fire. As someone has well said, *"Any old bush will do."*

HOLY GROUND

"And He said, Do not come near: put off your shoes from off your feet, for the place whereon you stand is holy ground" (Ex. 3:5).

Wherever God is, that place is holy, and it's holy only as long as God is there.

Any time the Lord appears for any reason, it is always for a purpose. I think it can be said without fear of exaggeration that the purpose, in one way or the other, is always deliverance. It was time for the children of Israel to be delivered.

Whatever it is that God is to do, He always uses people. Moses would be His instrument at that present time.

As well, that which He assigns to His human instrument is always impossible in the natural. In other words, the person must have God and His power in order to accomplish the task.

The ground was rendered holy by the presence of God upon it.

Moses was born to be Israel's deliverer, and yet, he did not receive his commission until he was 80 years of age. His commission was about to be given. It began with a burning bush, which, incidentally, was not consumed because the fire was of the presence of God and then a voice out of that fire.

IS IT THE PLACE THAT IS HOLY?

The very first admonition given to Moses by God was for him to be aware of the holiness of the place because, as stated, God was there. So, his commission started out with holiness.

Men oftentimes get the situation backward. It was not the place that was holy, for there was nothing holy about it. It was God who made the place holy by His presence. It was holy only as long as the Lord was there.

Due to the fact that every true believer is a temple of the Holy Spirit, this means that every true believer is holy, but only because of the presence of the Lord. If we do not understand this and treat this holiness with contempt, the Scripture says: *"If any man defile the temple of God, him shall God destroy; for the temple of God is holy, which temple you are"* (I Cor. 3:17).

THE NEW COVENANT

This is what makes the new covenant of such great advantage over the old covenant. That which we are reading concerning Moses and the Lord speaking to him is, in fact, a constant thing with believers under the new covenant. Incidentally, the privilege of having the Spirit of God dwell within us on a constant basis, in effect, abiding forever (Jn. 14:16–17), is all made possible by what Jesus did at the Cross. There He paid the terrible sin debt owed by man to God, and did so totally and completely.

Concerning Christ, Paul said: *"But now has He* (Christ) *obtained a more excellent ministry, by how much also He is the mediator of a better covenant, which was established upon better promises* (which He did by the Cross)" (Heb. 8:6).

The holiness that is mentioned in Exodus 3:5 could not be translated per se to human beings before the Cross. The blood of animal sacrifices could not cleanse from sin. It served a purpose, which was to point to the One who was to come. This *better covenant,* based on *better promises,* could only come about through a *better sacrifice* (Heb. 9:12–14).

I'm trying to bring out the point that through and by the Cross, we now have much better advantages even than did the great Moses.

WHY WAS MOSES REQUIRED TO PULL OFF HIS SHOES?

Joshua was required to do the same thing (Josh. 5:15).

Once again we come back to the Cross. Before the Cross, man was contaminated. The blood of bulls and goats could not take away sins; therefore, the sin debt still hung over even the greatest among the prophets.

Now, due to the Cross and the Holy Spirit abiding within believers permanently, in a sense, all that is about the child of God, at least those things which are legitimate, are made holy as well.

In Old Testament times, if a man were selling a piece of property, or as a kinsman redeemer, he was giving up his right to purchase a certain piece of land, he would pull off his shoe and give it to the one who bought the land. This meant that he was relinquishing all claims.

When the Lord asked that Moses pull off his shoes, and He asked the same thing of Joshua, their doing so signified that they were relinquishing all claims, and that they belonged solely to the Lord (Ruth 4:6–9).

THE GOD OF ABRAHAM, THE GOD OF ISAAC, AND THE GOD OF JACOB

"Moreover He said, I am the God of your father, the God of Abraham, the God of Isaac, and the God of Jacob.

And Moses hid his face; for he was afraid to look upon God" (Ex. 3:6).

The word *father,* as it is used here, refers to forefathers in general.

Jesus used this verse (Mat. 22:32) to confirm the resurrection. He referred to these three and then stated, *"God is not the God of the dead, but of the living."*

In essence, He was saying that these men, plus all who have trusted God, were not dead but alive. In fact, at the moment that the Lord spoke to Moses and, as well, as Christ spoke to the crowd of His day, these three men, plus all other believers, were in paradise in the heart of the earth. They were there awaiting the victory that would be won at the Cross when, in actuality, Jesus would deliver them from that place and take them to heaven (Eph. 4:8). Since the Cross, all believers immediately go to be with Christ in heaven (Phil. 1:23).

I AM

As far as we know, this appearance by God to Moses was the first appearance since Jacob's going down into Egypt about 215 years before.

If it is to be noticed, the Lord didn't say, *"I 'was' the God of Abraham, Isaac, and Jacob,"* but *"I 'am,'"* proving that the patriarchs were still alive, even though they had died physically a long time before. The soul and the spirit of man never die and will spend eternity either with the Lord or in everlasting darkness.

Moses hiding his face was because of the holiness of God. Each laborer in the vineyard needs to keep constantly before him the fact that the One with whom he is associated and the One whom he serves is holy, in fact, thrice-holy. A realization of this will check the lightness and levity of the flesh.

AFFLICTION

"And the LORD said, I have surely seen the affliction of My people which are in Egypt, and have heard their cry by reason of their taskmasters; for I know their sorrows" (Ex. 3:7).

The children of Israel in Egypt were a perfect type of the condition of the natural man who is the bondslave of sin and the captive of Satan. This is true not only of the slave of lust or the helpless victim of drugs, etc., but, as well, of the moral and refined. They, too, are in bondage to selfish desire, self-will, pleasure, ambition, greed, unforgiveness, etc.

Pink says: *"The 'affliction' which sin has brought is everywhere to be seen, not only in physical suffering, but as well, in mental restlessness and heart discontent."*

The varied lusts of the flesh are just as merciless as the Egyptian taskmasters of old, and the sorrows of sin's slaves today just as acute as those of the Israelites in the midst of the iron furnace of Egypt.

Pink went on to say: *"What woe there really is behind the fair surface of society! How fearful the misery which has come on the whole race of man through sin! How great the need for the Saviour! How terrible the guilt of despising Him now that He has come!"*

However, even though Verse 7 of Chapter 3 of Exodus vividly portrays the state of the unredeemed, if the believer doesn't understand God's prescribed order of victory through the Cross, he can find himself ruled over by the sin nature exactly as he was before conversion.

GOD'S PRESCRIBED ORDER OF VICTORY

In Chapter 6 of Romans, the Apostle Paul outlines to us God's method of sanctification, and we might say, how to have victory over the flesh, or how that we may perpetually keep the sin nature in check.

The Lord has only one way of victory, and that is the way of the Cross.

To explain this which the Lord has done for us, the Holy Spirit through Paul first takes us to the Cross. He said: *"Don't you know, that so many of us as were baptized into Jesus Christ were baptized into His death?*

"Therefore we are buried with Him by baptism into death: that like as Christ was raised up from the dead by the glory of the Father, even so we also should walk in newness of life.

"For if we have been planted together in the likeness of His death, we shall be also in the likeness of His resurrection" (Rom. 6:3–5).

Most Christians brush across these passages simply because they think that Paul is speaking here of water baptism. Concluding that they have been baptized in water, they do not at all see the tremendous statement that is being made here.

Paul is not speaking of water baptism; in fact, he doesn't have water baptism in mind, as important as that ordinance actually is.

He is speaking of the crucifixion of Christ, how He died, was buried, and then raised from the dead, and our dying with Him, being buried with Him, and then being raised with Him.

We must realize that everything Christ did was done in totality for us and not at all for Himself. He didn't come down here to die on a Cross for heaven, for God the Father, for the Holy Spirit, for angels, or Himself, as stated, but altogether for sinners, i.e., for us. Jesus Christ was actually our substitute, who Paul referred to as the *"last Adam"* (I Cor. 15:45). The term, *last Adam,* is used because the work that Jesus would accomplish at the Cross would be so total, so complete, and so final that there would never be the need of another Adam. Where the first Adam failed, the last Adam succeeded in every capacity.

The fall of the first Adam took everyone down with him, and we speak of all of humanity yet to be born. Due to the fall, all would be born in original sin, therefore, without God, dead in trespasses and sins.

However, as the first Adam knocked us down, the last Adam, the Lord Jesus Christ, picked us up. As we were lost through the first Adam, we are saved through the last Adam.

HOW ARE WE SAVED?

Paul answered that, as well: *"For by grace are you saved through faith; and that not of yourselves: it is the gift of God: "Not of works, lest any man should boast"* (Eph. 2:8–9).

We are all saved through the goodness of God, which is defined as *"grace,"* and it is brought about through an exhibition of faith on our part (Jn. 3:16).

In other words, when the believing sinner exhibits faith in Christ, as far as God is concerned, that believing sinner is actually placed into Christ, in His death, His burial, and His resurrection. That's what Paul was talking about when he said, *"we are baptized into His death."* He used the word *baptized* because it's the strongest word that can be used to explain what the apostle meant. He meant that Christ is in us, and we are in Christ. It's like a ship that has sunk to the bottom of the sea. The water is in the ship, and the ship is in the water, which is an excellent symbol of the word *baptize* or *baptism.* That's what we are in Christ. Jesus said: *"At that day* (after He went to the Cross, and the Holy Spirit was sent back) *you shall know that I am in My Father, and you in Me, and I in you"* (Jn. 14:20).

NEWNESS OF LIFE

So, when Christ died, we died with Him. In fact, there had to be a death on our part. As I'm sure the reader knows, I'm not speaking of physical death, but yet, Jesus definitely did die physically. However, our death is that which happens in the spiritual when we die to the old man (the old way), what we once were.

Man's problem is that he keeps trying to improve the old man. It cannot be done. There is no such thing as moral evolution. In fact, it is the very opposite. Despite all of the thousands of years of education and technological advancement, still, men are slaughtering each other today even worse than ever.

We were then buried with Christ, which means that all of what we once were, which speaks of sin, iniquity, transgression, etc., were buried with Him.

We were then raised with Him in *"newness of life,"* actually, a new creation, with old things having passed away and all things having become new (II Cor. 5:17).

All of this which I have described is actually the born-again experience.

THE SIN NATURE

However, even though we are now born again, and even Spirit-filled, the sin nature within us doesn't die. It remains, but it is dormant! The Scripture says that we are *"dead to the sin nature"* because of what Christ did at the Cross. Paul said: *"Likewise reckon you also yourselves to be dead indeed unto the sin* (sin nature), *but alive unto God through Jesus Christ our Lord"* (Rom. 6:11).

In this one verse of Scripture, we find the manner in which we are to believe, i.e., to exhibit our faith, in other words, what the correct object of our faith ought to be. This is very, very important, as we've already briefly discussed.

We are *"dead indeed unto the sin"* nature because we died with Christ on the Cross. It's as simple as that.

No, we were not there when Christ died, but our faith in Him, at least in the mind of God, puts us there.

If you are to notice, in quoting Verse 11, I used the term, *the sin.* In the original text as Paul wrote it, he used in front of the word *sin* that which is referred to as the definite article. In other words, he said, *"Dead indeed unto the sin."* Sin is used here as a noun, which means that he's not referring to particular acts of sin, but rather to the sin nature.

Now, once again, notice that Paul didn't say that the sin nature was dead, but rather that we are dead unto the sin nature.

WHAT IS THE SIN NATURE?

The sin nature is what Adam and Eve became immediately upon their fall. It meant that their very nature became that of sin, meaning that every single thing they did was from wrong motives, which God labeled as sin. Their nature became sin, which means that they were controlled by the sin nature. Due to the fact that all of us were in Adam, this means that every single individual is born with a sin nature. As well, we must understand that it is impossible to improve the sin nature. In fact, it is the very opposite that takes place, meaning that the sin nature becomes worse and worse as time goes by. There's only one solution for this terrible blight of darkness with which every human being must contend, and that is Jesus Christ.

That's the reason the modern church is so foolish as to embrace humanistic psychology as the answer to man's dilemma. Such not only cannot help, it actually hurts.

When the believing sinner comes to Christ, while the sin nature is not removed, it is, as we have stated, made dormant. It's like an electrical appliance that is unplugged. In that condition, it can do no harm; however, sadly and regrettably, the sin nature can quickly have a revival. Let's look at another question before we go further with this.

WHY DOESN'T THE LORD REMOVE THE SIN NATURE WHEN THE BELIEVING SINNER IS BORN AGAIN?

The fact is, He doesn't!

The only answer I've been able to ascertain is that the Lord allows the sin nature to remain in order that it may serve as a disciplinarian. In other words, if we leave God's true way, which is faith in Christ and what He did for us at the Cross, we will find the sin nature reviving. So, the Lord allows it to remain to discipline us.

In fact, there will come an hour that the sin nature will be totally, completely, and forever removed. It will be when the trump of God sounds. The Scripture says: *"For this corruptible* (the sin nature) *must put on incorruption* (a glorified body with no sin nature), *and this mortal* (subject to death) *must put on immortality* (will never die)" (I Cor. 15:53).

This means that the glorified saints of God will not have a sin nature and will not be subject to death or even aging.

HOW DOES THE BELIEVER STAY DEAD TO THE SIN NATURE?

That's the great question!

We remain dead to the sin nature by continuing to exhibit faith on a daily basis in Christ and what Christ has done for us at the Cross (Lk. 9:23). Being dead means that the sin nature no longer bothers us, which means that we're living victoriously over the world, the flesh, and the Devil. We must never separate Christ from the Cross or the Cross from Christ. That is where our victory was won, and that's where our victory remains.

This means that the glorified saints of God will not have a sin nature and will not be subject to death or even aging.

Now, this is where Satan will do everything within his power to hinder us. This is what Paul was talking about when he told Timothy: *"Fight the good fight of faith, lay hold on eternal life, whereunto you are also called, and have professed a good profession before many witnesses"* (I Tim. 6:12). The good fight of faith is the fight we are supposed to fight, and it's the only fight that we are supposed to fight. Satan is ever trying to move our faith from the Cross to other things, and he doesn't too much care what the other things are. This means we have to fight to keep the Cross as the object of our faith.

DOMINION

Christians are running around trying to increase their faith when that's not the problem. The problem is having one's faith in the wrong object. The correct object must always be the Cross of Christ. If it's something else, then we're going to have problems (Rom. 6:1-14; I Cor. 1:17, 18, 23; 2:2; Gal. 6:14; Col. 2:10-15).

The Holy Spirit will function within our hearts and lives only as we stay within the boundaries of the Cross, and that means to maintain our faith in that finished work (Gal. 6:14). By maintaining our faith in the Cross, the Holy Spirit will then work mightily upon our behalf, which ensures us of victory (Rom. 8:1–2, 11).

Maintaining our faith in the correct object will guarantee that *"sin shall not have dominion over you"* (Rom. 6:14). While the Bible does not teach sinless perfection, it definitely does teach that sin is not to dominate us.

Concerning dominion, Paul also said: *"Let not sin* (the sin nature) *therefore reign* (rule) *in your mortal body* (showing that the sin nature can once again rule in the heart and life of the believer, if the believer doesn't constantly look to Christ and the Cross; the mortal body is neutral, which means it can be used for righteousness or unrighteousness), *that you should obey it in the lusts thereof* (ungodly lusts are carried out through the mortal body, if faith is not maintained in the Cross [I Cor. 1:17-18]).

"*Neither yield you your members* (of your mortal body) *as instruments of unrighteousness unto sin* (the sin nature): *but yield yourselves unto God* (we are to yield ourselves to Christ and the Cross; that alone guarantees victory over the sin nature), *as those who are alive from the dead* (we have been raised with Christ in 'newness of life'), *and your members* (members of our physical body) *as instruments of righteousness unto God* (this can be done only by virtue of the Cross and our faith in that finished work, and faith which continues in that finished work from day to day [Lk. 9:23-24]).

"*For sin shall not have dominion over you* (the sin nature will not have dominion over us if we as believers continue to exercise faith in the Cross of Christ; otherwise, the sin nature most definitely will have dominion over the believer): *for you are not under the law* (means that if we try to live this life by any type of law, no matter how good that law might be in its own right, we will conclude by the sin nature having dominion over us), *but under grace* (the grace of God flows to the believer on an unending basis only as long as the believer exercises faith in Christ and what He did at the Cross; grace is merely the goodness of God exercised by and through the Holy Spirit, and given to undeserving saints)" (Rom. 6:12-14).

LAW AND GRACE

What did Paul mean by the statement, *"For you are not under the law, but under grace"*? (Rom. 6:14).

He meant that we are no longer living in the dispensation of law, but rather the dispensation of grace. The law was always meant to be temporary, and it always pointed to Christ who was to come. When Jesus came, He fulfilled the law in every respect. Now it is no more binding upon believers.

What Paul meant was, while the law told men what they ought to do, it gave them no power to do it. That's the difference in law and grace.

Grace shows us what is right, as well, exactly as the law did, but at the same time, it gives us power to do what we ought to do, which the law never could do. That's the difference in law and grace. I might quickly add, that difference is great.

Please read this carefully because it's very, very important: The way that the believer is to have grace within his life is that we look exclusively to Christ and the Cross. That being done, the Holy Spirit will see to it that the grace of God, which is the goodness of God, flows to us in an unending stream. Grace is simply the goodness of God extended to undeserving people.

The way that we are guaranteed an unending supply of grace is by our faith remaining constantly in Christ and the Cross. The believer must understand that it is the Cross of Christ that has made, and does make, grace possible for all believers. Unfortunately, most Christians are functioning in law instead of grace. They don't mean to do that, but that's what is happening.

WHY DO WE SAY THAT MOST CHRISTIANS ARE FUNCTIONING IN LAW?

Sadly, we say it because it is true.

The reason I know this is because most Christians do not have the faintest idea as to the working of the Cross of Christ in our everyday living for God. They understand the Cross to a certain degree, meaning that they refer to it as being absolutely necessary for our salvation, which is correct. However, once they are saved, the Cross in the modern church is by and large ignored. Please understand that I'm speaking here not of mere benchwarmers, but rather those who truly are born again, who truly love the Lord, and who are Spirit-filled and want to please God. But yet, they are living in a state of law, which cannot please God.

The Cross of Christ has as much to do with our everyday living for God as it did for our initial salvation. To receive its benefit, which is the grace of God in an unending flow, it only remains for us to understand that every single thing that we receive from God is made possible by the Cross of Christ. When I say everything we receive from God, I mean all and without exception. In other words, the Cross is the means by which all of these great things are done. It remains then for our faith to be anchored exclusively in Christ and what He did for us at the Cross, and to do so on a constant basis (Rom. 6:1-14; 8:1-11; I Cor. 1:17, 18, 23; 2:2; Col. 2:10-15).

The Holy Spirit is God, who can do anything. When the believer's faith is anchored squarely in Christ and the Cross, and maintained in Christ and the Cross, the Holy Spirit will work mightily on our behalf.

THE HOLY SPIRIT AND THE CROSS

It is the Cross of Christ that gave and gives the legal means to the Holy Spirit for Him to do all that He does. Please understand that it is the Cross that has made it all possible, and makes it all possible. The Holy Spirit will not work outside of those boundaries of the Cross of Christ. In fact, that's a law.

The Word says: *"The law of the Spirit of life in Christ Jesus has made me free from the law of sin and death"* (Rom. 8:2).

As I've stated, this is a law, meaning it was devised by the Godhead in eternity past, and it will function exactly as it has been designed.

The short phrase, *"in Christ Jesus,"* which was used by Paul in one manner or the other some 170 times in his 14 epistles, refers totally and completely to the Cross. In other words, it's speaking of what Jesus there did. As repeatedly stated, when we talk about the Cross, we aren't speaking of the wooden beam on which Jesus died, but rather what He there accomplished.

WHAT DID JESUS ACCOMPLISH AT THE CROSS?

Everything!

He atoned for all sin — past, present, and future — at least for all who will believe (Jn. 3:16). He did so by giving His perfect body as a perfect sacrifice, which effected a perfect redemption. When He did that, and God the Father accepted it, this atoned for all sin, as stated, past, present, and future.

Sin is the fuel, so to speak, which gives Satan the right, and we mean the legal right, to hold man captive. However, with all sin atoned, he has no more legal right to hold anyone in bondage. So, if that is the case, and considering that Jesus has atoned for all sin, how is it that most of the world is still in bondage?

It is because the unredeemed world will not take advantage of what Christ did at the Cross, and they continue to try to carve out their own salvation, that is, if they believe in any type of salvation at all. So, their sin remains because they do not believe, and it gives Satan a continued legal means to hold them captive.

However, then we come to the believer. Sad to say, most believers fall into the same category. They are not taking advantage of what Jesus did at the Cross, still trying to formulate some type of victory by engaging themselves in all manner of works. This gives Satan the legal means to continue holding them in bondage.

It is sad, but virtually all of the modern church — and again, we speak of those who truly love the Lord — are captives to the sin nature, continually struggling, trying to over-come something in their lives that's impossible to do.

Let me say it again: There's only one answer for sin, and to be sure, sin is the problem. That answer is the Cross of Christ.

Paul said: *"But this Man* (this priest, Christ Jesus), *after He had offered one sacrifice for sins forever* (speaks of the Cross), *sat down on the right hand of God* (refers to the great contrast with the priests under the Levitical system, who never sat down because their work was never com-pleted; the work of Christ was a finished work and needed no repetition, hence, him sitting down at the right hand of God)" (Heb. 10:12).

So, if we attempt to address sin in any manner other than by the Cross of Christ, the result is always failure. That's the reason that humanistic psychology is that which will not work. Not only will it not work, it actually harms the indi-vidual. The answer is Jesus Christ and Him crucified.

The believer must plant his faith exclusively in Christ and the Cross, and maintain it exclusively in Christ and the Cross, understanding that the Cross of Christ is the means by which everything is given to us. If he does this, he will then find the Holy Spirit helping him in ways he never thought possible. This is God's way, and His only way, because no other way is needed.

The Cross is the answer to victory or the lack thereof. It is the answer for the bondages of darkness. It is the answer for satanic powers. There is no other answer, as there can be no other answer!

AFFLICTION

Before we go to the next verse, let's look at affliction a little more.

Egypt was a type of the world. To be sure, had the Israelites remained comfortable in Egypt as they had been under Joseph, they simply would not have wanted to leave. It is the same with the modern believer.

While we as believers are definitely in the world, the world definitely is not to be in us. However, that's the great problem.

The Lord is fashioning us into the heavenly image. First, the believing sinner must be born again, which typifies the deliverance of the children of Israel from Egyptian bondage. Then the training begins.

It was the Cross that got the children of Israel out of Egypt, and it is the Cross that got us out of the dominion of the world. Also, it was the Cross that instituted Israel's training, and it is the same with us presently.

However, the sadness is, most Christians, knowing little about the Cross, understand it only in the capacity of their initial salvation experience. Beyond that, they draw a blank.

Not understanding the Cross regarding their sanctification, they attempt to bring this about by their own ability, strength, and machinations. Then, they embark on the long road of failure, for there is no victory in self.

VICTORY

God doesn't give victory to men in general or man in particular. He gives all victory to Christ. The victory that we have, which we can surely have in abundance, must come through our association with Christ and Christ alone. This is done by evidencing faith in Christ and His sufferings (Gal. 1:4).

All of this I've stated may seem to be very simple on the surface; however, due to the problems of self and the flesh, it can become very complicated. Oftentimes, affliction is necessary before we will finally cry unto the Lord as we should and, thereby, come to a place of total dependence on Him. The truth is, the Christian will cling to the flesh as long as there is any flesh left. All hope of the flesh must be gone before the believer will totally look to Christ.

However, in the meantime, all believers think they're looking to Christ and will proclaim vigorously that they are definitely looking to Christ. As stated, the truth is, as long as any part of the flesh remains, and we continue to speak of self, the believer will cling to the last shred, while much of the time thinking that he's clinging to Christ.

WHY DOES PAUL DEAL WITH THE FLESH SO MUCH?

He does so because the flesh is the problem.

As we've already explained, the flesh is that which pertains to the ability of a human being. In other words, it is our talent, education, motivation, willpower, personal strength, etc., i.e. what a human being can do.

These things are not really sin within themselves, but we make sin out of them when we try to live for God by the means of education, motivation, willpower, etc.

Due to the fall in the garden of Eden, man has been rendered incapable of doing what he must do. So, the fact is, we simply cannot live for God, cannot be what we ought to be, and cannot have victory in our hearts and lives over sin by the means of the flesh. It just simply cannot be done.

So, the Lord has made a way for us to walk in victory, and that way is the Cross of Christ. This is something that anyone can do, and we speak of having faith in Christ and the Cross. It doesn't matter whether they are old or young, rich or poor, great or small, red, yellow, brown, black, white, etc. It doesn't matter the nationality, and it doesn't matter the creed or the culture. The design of victory as God has given it, which is the Cross of Christ, can be engaged by anyone. It only takes faith.

We must understand that for every single thing we receive from God, Jesus Christ is the source.

As well, we must understand that the Cross of Christ is the means, and the only means, by which all of these things are given to us.

With our faith anchored squarely in the Cross of Christ, and maintained in the Cross of Christ, the Holy Spirit will then work mightily on our behalf, without which, we simply cannot live this life. Now, that's God way, and His only way, because no other way is needed.

But yet, every single believer who has ever lived has tried to live for God by the means of the flesh. Almost all have done so simply because they didn't know any better.

For instance, when you read Chapter 7 of Romans, you are reading the experience of Paul the apostle after he was saved, Spirit-filled, and preaching the gospel. He tried to live the life that he knew he should live but simply couldn't do it. He stated, *"For that which I do* (the failure) *I allow not* (should have been translated, 'I understand not'; these are not the words of an unsaved man, as some claim, but rather a believer who is trying and failing): *for what I would, that do I not* (refers to the obedience he wants to render to Christ, but rather fails; why? as Paul explained, the believer is married to Christ but is being unfaithful to Christ by spiritually cohabiting with the law, which frustrates the grace of God; that means the Holy Spirit will not help such a person, which guarantees failure [Gal. 2:21]); *but what I hate, that do I* (refers to sin in his life which he doesn't want to do and, in fact, hates, but finds himself unable to stop; unfortunately, due to the fact of not understanding the Cross as it refers to sanctification, this is the plight of most modern Christians)" (Rom. 7:15).

To be sure, when Paul wrote this, he was walking in total victory. He had found the secret of the Cross and was living therein. However, for a period of time, how long we do not know but possibly several years, Paul walked in defeat because he did not understand at that time God's prescribed order of victory.

As well, we might quickly add, there was no one else in the world at that time that understood this great avenue of victory, the Cross. In fact, it was to Paul that this great truth was given. Jesus Christ is the new covenant, and the Cross of Christ is the meaning of that covenant, the meaning of which was given to the Apostle Paul (Gal. 1:12).

Every true believer hates sin. While the flesh may want something that's wrong, the inward man doesn't want that which is wrong. Paul also said: *"For I delight in the law of God* (refers to the moral law of God ensconced in the Ten Commandments) *after the inward man* (refers to the spirit and soul of man which has now been regenerated)" (Rom. 7:22).

So, let us say it again. Every true believer hates sin, and rightly so. As well, we must understand the following also: Most of the time, the wrongdoing that is committed by believers is not the real problem. The real problem is what caused the wrongdoing. What caused it is the believer (many times through ignorance) trying to live for God by the means of the flesh. No matter how hard we try, such an effort is doomed to failure. Now, read that again and read it carefully.

When we try to live for God by the means of the flesh, which is by our own ability and strength, we are doomed to failure.

Now, many would retort that they are trusting Christ and not trying to live by the means of the flesh, etc.

However, let me counter by saying this: Unless the believer understands the Cross of Christ as it refers to our everyday living for God, in other words, the great part the Cross plays in all of this, no matter what the believer may do, he is going to function in the flesh. There are only two ways to go, and that is law or grace. Law functions through the flesh, while grace functions through the Holy Spirit. This means that law is guaranteed of failure, and the Holy Spirit is guaranteed of victory.

CHRIST AND HIM CRUCIFIED

Why did Paul use the term in Galatians 2:20: *"I am crucified with Christ"*?

He did so for this reason: The only way that the believer can truly cling to Christ, truly trust Christ, truly depend on Christ, and truly look to Christ for all things is to place his faith and confidence in what Christ has done at the Cross. To try to trust Christ in any other fashion concludes by the person serving *"another Jesus"* (II Cor. 11:4). While the *"other Jesus"* may look like the real thing and, thereby, make us believe it's the real thing, there will be no positive, scriptural results from such a union.

"Another Jesus," as Paul put it, always, and without exception, refers to Christ apart from the Cross. While Christ is definitely a healing Jesus, we must always understand that the healings come to us strictly through what Christ did at the Cross (I Pet. 2:24). While Christ is definitely a *"blessing Jesus,"* once again, we must always understand that such blessings come, without exception, through the Cross (Eph. 1:3). While Christ is definitely the baptizer with the Holy Spirit, He is that simply because of what He has done at the

Cross (Mat. 3:11; Jn. 7:37–39). It is the Cross which makes everything possible, and until we understand that and place our faith in Christ and what He did for us in His finished work, we will never know victory. So, affliction is often needed to bring us to the place we ought to be.

It's not that the affliction carries within itself any type of power or grace, for it doesn't. However, it does tend to force the issue by having us look totally to Christ and His finished work, thereby, forsaking our dependence on the flesh.

DELIVERANCE

"And I am come down to deliver them out of the hand of the Egyptians, and to bring them up out of that land unto a good land and a large, unto a land flowing with milk and honey; unto the place of the Canaanites, and the Hittites, and the Amorites, and the Perizzites, and the Hivites, and the Jebusites" (Ex. 3:8).

Before we look at the delivering aspect, let's look at this land to which the Lord would bring His people. To be sure, it was better, much better, than the land of Egypt. In Egypt, they only had a part of Goshen, whereas the entirety of the land of Canaan was approximately 60,000 square miles. It was truly a *"good land and a large"* (I Ki. 4:20–21).

Eastward of Jordan, the soil is very rich and productive, with vast tracts producing enormous crops of grain. Throughout the year, there is pasturage of every kind in abundance.

The phrase, *"flowing with milk and honey,"* which was first used here and is so common in the later books (Num. 13:27; Deut. 26:9, 15; 31:20; Jer. 11:5; 32:22; Ezek. 20:6, etc.), was a proverbial expression for *"a land of plenty."*

The point of all of this is, what they were being given was far greater than what they were leaving. It is the same with the modern believer and the world. What the Lord brings us out of is far less (much less) than that which He brings us into. In fact, there is no comparison.

MODERN BELIEVERS

As it regards Verse 8 of Chapter 3 of Exodus, what you the believer are reading was meant not only for the Israelites of so long ago, but is meant for every believer presently and, in fact, much more.

Whatever God promised Israel before the law and after the law, He promises so much more presently.

Listen to what Paul said: *"But now* (since the Cross) *has He* (the Lord Jesus) *obtained a more excellent ministry* (the new covenant in Jesus' blood is superior and takes the place of the old covenant in animal blood), *by how much also He is the mediator of a better covenant* (proclaims the fact that Christ officiates between God and man according to the arrangements of the new covenant), *which was established upon better promises.* (This presents the new covenant, explicitly based on the cleansing and forgiveness of all sin, which the old covenant could not do.)

"For if that first covenant had been faultless (proclaims the fact that the first covenant was definitely not faultless; as stated, it was based on animal blood, which was vastly inferior to the precious blood of Christ), *then should no place have been sought for the second* (proclaims the necessity of the new covenant)" (Heb. 8:6-7).

All of this means that whatever the Lord did for Israel of old, He will do more, much more, much, much more now under the new covenant. The only reason we don't have it is simply because we don't believe for it.

When I was a kid coming up in a small Full gospel church, I heard preachers say, *"God blessed Israel materially, but God doesn't do that now."* Nothing could be further from the truth.

The Lord wants to bless you abundantly in the material sense (which refers to the financial), in the physical sense, and in the spiritual sense. As we've just stated, the reason we don't have it, whatever it is, is simply because we don't believe for it. The promise is plainly given to us that we now have a better covenant based on better promises. Now, if that is true, and it most definitely is, then whatever He gave to Israel long, long ago, He will do so now, and even in a much greater way.

Every believer on the face of the earth should believe God to be blessed financially. We should believe God to be blessed physically, and above all, we should believe God to be blessed spiritually. The new covenant is full of promises to this effect.

Listen to our Lord: *"For verily I say unto you, that whosoever shall say unto this mountain, Be thou removed, and be thou cast into the sea; and shall not doubt in his heart, but shall believe that those things which he says shall come to pass; he shall have whatsoever he says"* (Mk. 11:23).

And then, *"Therefore I say unto you, What things soever you desire, when you pray, believe that you receive them, and you shall have them"* (Mk. 11:24).

Now, did He mean what He said or not?

"And all things, whatsoever you shall ask in prayer, believing, you shall receive" (Mat. 21:22).

"If then God so clothe the grass, which is today in the field, and tomorrow as cast into the oven; how much more will He clothe you, O ye of little faith?

"And seek not what you shall eat, or what you shall drink, neither be ye of doubtful mind.

"For all these things do the nations of the world seek after: and your Father knows that you have need of these things.

"But rather seek ye the kingdom of God; and all these things shall be added unto you.

"Fear not, little flock; for it is your Father's good pleasure to give you the kingdom" (Lk. 12:28-32).

"If you abide in Me, and My words abide in you, you shall ask what you will, and it shall be done unto you" (Jn. 15:7).

"If you shall ask anything in My name, I will do it" (Jn. 14:14).

"But my God shall supply all your need according to His riches in glory by Christ Jesus" (Phil. 4:19).

"But this I say, He which sows sparingly shall reap also sparingly; and he which sows bountifully shall reap also bountifully" (II Cor. 9:6).

"Give, and it shall be given unto you; good measure, pressed down, and shaken together, and running over, shall men give into your bosom. For with the same measure that you mete withal it shall be measured to you again" (Lk. 6:38).

These are only a few promises in the Word of God, and the question is, *"Do we believe that God meant what He said?"* Every believer should claim these promises in every capacity, not only in the spiritual. To be sure, the Lord will do exactly what He said He will do.

THE ASPECT OF DELIVERANCE

The phrase, *"And I am come down to deliver them out of the hand of the Egyptians,"* reveals a great fundamental principle regarding the ways of God. It is on the ground of what He is that He ever acts, and not on the ground of what the people are as it regards righteousness, etc.

Actually, the children of Israel in Egypt were not paragons of virtue and righteousness. In fact, they were the very opposite. For them even to exhibit a little faith, they had to be brought to a place of terrible bondage. So, the delivering aspect had to do with God's promises to Abraham, Isaac, and Jacob, which constitutes who He is and what He is. If the Lord waited until we were worthy of deliverance, He would never act simply because no human being has ever reached that place. He only requires faith, and for faith to be had and exhibited, in some way, the Word of God must be sent to the people, even as it was under Moses. Then it was affliction that drove them to the place of exhibiting their faith.

It is the same with us presently. There is no merit in us that triggers deliverance, but yet, it's hard for us to come to that place to where we cease to look to ourselves and, thereby, look totally to God.

THE SHED BLOOD OF THE LAMB

As we will see, even as the text progresses chapter by chapter, the factor and the principle which ultimately delivered Israel was the shed blood of the lamb. All the miracles that God performed only set the stage. They really effected no deliverance. It was totally and completely the Cross of Christ, registered in the symbolism of the slain lamb, which brought Egypt to her knees and victory to Israel.

As we go through this text, let the reader understand that as it was with Israel of old, it is presently with believers and, in fact, always has been. There is no saving grace, no delivering grace, and no healing grace outside of the Cross.

If I weary the reader by my constant, even overbearing attention to the Cross, I do so for a purpose. The church has been moved so far away from the Cross that it no longer understands its place and position of life and victory. It is so bogged down in legalism, Galatianism, or even the opposite, which is antinomianism, that it has completely lost sight of victory.

LEGALISM, GALATIANISM, AND ANTINOMIANISM

In brief, legalism pertains to salvation by works, which, in reality, doesn't exist.

Galatianism, which afflicts most of the modern church, pertains to believers who come to Christ by trusting in what He has done for us at the Cross, and then trying to live for God by their own strength and ability, in other words, abandoning the Cross. In that capacity, it is salvation by faith and sanctification by works, which will never succeed.

Antinomianism is the very opposite in that it claims that sin no longer matters inasmuch as we are now functioning in grace. In other words, *"Where sin abounded, grace did much more abound,"* so I don't have to worry anymore about how much I might sin. Of course, that road is a road to disaster. In one of these three, the majority of the modern church now resides.

All of it is a failure to understand the Cross, and so, that's the reason I address this subject from every angle I know, even to the place of tedious repetition, in order that the reader will not fail to see what is being said.

ENEMIES IN THE LAND

If it is to be noticed, the Lord mentioned the fact that there would be Canaanites, Hittites, etc., in the land. Of course, we speak of the land that the Lord would give to His people.

This refers to the enemies of the soul which seek to drag down the child of God after having come into the Land of

Promise, so to speak. Despite the fact that much modern teaching on faith claims that if we have the proper confession, there will be no difficulties or problems, we find to our dismay that we still have to face the Canaanites, etc. Denying their existence doesn't make them go away, and ignoring them does not provide a place of security and peace. As we shall see, when we come to the book of Joshua, this great soldier of the Lord had to defeat these enemies, which he did. The believer must understand that the Land of Promise is not necessarily the land of possession.

Let's say it in another way: It's a whole lot easier to receive the promise than it is to have the possession. However, it definitely can be had, and if we follow that which the Lord has given us, and do so faithfully, we definitely will possess all that Jesus has provided for us.

A GREAT DIFFERENCE

As it regards Joshua, along with the judges and David, etc., these men served as types of Christ. The victories they won were types of the victories won for us by Jesus Christ.

However, the problem that the modern saint faces is misunderstanding the possession of the land. He tries to do all over again what Christ has already done. Jesus Christ has totally and completely defeated every single power of darkness. To use the vernacular of Exodus, He has defeated the Canaanites, the Hivites, the Jebusites, etc., which means that we don't have to defeat them, but this is where the Christian slips up. He keeps trying to fight a fight that's already been fought and won, attempting to effect a victory that has already been accomplished. Let me hurriedly say that if we attempt to do that, we will be defeated every single time. There has never been one single winner in this type of conflict. The reasons are many and obvious.

THE FINISHED WORK OF CHRIST

To try to fight a battle which has already been fought and won by Christ is an insult to Christ and, to be sure, a place and position in which the Holy Spirit will not function. Sadly and regrettably, the modern Christian engages in this conflict simply because he doesn't know or understand God's prescribed order of victory.

Under the new covenant, which is very, very important, in order to possess all that Christ has done for us, and I speak of this more abundant life (Jn. 10:10), all we have to do is exhibit faith in Christ. Yes, you know what I'm about to say next and what He did for us at the Cross. If we place our faith in that finished work and not allow it to be moved elsewhere, the Holy Spirit will then guarantee to us all that Christ has done for us (Col. 2:10–15; Rom. 8:1–11).

PERSONAL

When it comes to fighting Canaanites, Jebusites, etc., most probably, I personally am one of the most experienced in the world. I realize that if every believer could read this, many would smile and say, *"Brother Swaggart, you may think you are, but my own experience tops even yours."* Quite possibly, that is true, but the further truth is, not a single one of us ever succeeded, as no one will ever succeed in that endeavor.

As we've already stated, to try to do all over again what Christ has already done, which we cannot do anyway, is an insult of the highest order to the Son of God. When we think about this, we must realize that everything He did, He did solely and completely for you and me. He didn't do it for Himself, for He needed no deliverance. Considering the great price that He paid, and then for us to try to engage this conflict all over again, it greatly belittles the sacrifice that He offered of Himself. While we certainly don't mean to insult Him, that's actually what we are doing. In effect, it is the same as Cain offering up the labor of his own hands in sacrifice to God, which, of course, God could never accept (Gen., Chpt. 4).

God's way is the way of the Cross. That has always been His way, is His way now, and will be His way tomorrow.

The believer is to place his faith exclusively in Christ and what Christ did for us at the Cross, and maintain it there consistently, which will then enable the Holy Spirit to do what only He can do. We must ever understand that the Holy Spirit works exclusively within the realm of the finished work of Christ. In fact, He will not work outside of that capacity (Rom. 6:1-14; I Cor. 1:17, 18, 23; 2:2; Gal. 6:14; Col. 2:10-15).

A DELIVERANCE PREACHER?

Regrettably, most of the modern church completely misunderstands deliverance. The denominational church world little thinks of it at all for reasons which I will not now address. Most Pentecostals and Charismatics misunderstand the manner of deliverance, thinking somehow that preachers can deliver people, etc.

We try to do this by the laying on of hands, which, within itself, is very scriptural, but when used in this fashion, becomes unscriptural.

A few nights ago, I was watching a preacher for a few moments over television. His entire motif was to bring people before him, and him lay his hands on them, which was supposed to deliver them of their problems. Some of these people were needing healing, in which case, the laying on of hands is very scriptural. Others maybe just wanted to be blessed, which, as well, is scriptural. However, with those who were troubled by sins of some nature, bondages of some nature, etc., laying on of hands, at least in that fashion, will not help.

THE TRUTH WILL MAKE YOU FREE

Think about it a moment: Jesus said, *"You shall know the truth, and the truth shall make you free"* (Jn. 8:32).

It's the truth that people need, and that truth is the Cross of Christ.

If it could bring about deliverance for the individual, then Jesus didn't need to come down here and die on the Cross. No! The preacher, as well as thousands just like him, was drawing attention to himself instead of Christ. I'm not saying that he meant to do that, and I'm not even questioning his motives, rather believing that those motives were very good. However, the end result will not be good.

Let's say, for the sake of argument, that the preacher is godly and sincere and that the people are sincere. Let's say that the Lord really blesses them, and they even *"fall out in the Spirit"* or have some other type of like manifestation. Even though all of this is wonderful and good and will definitely be a blessing to the child of God, when the believer gets up from the floor and walks outside, 15 minutes later or two or three weeks later, whatever, the same problem he had when he went to the preacher, he will find himself continuing to have. Why?

Did not the power of God move on him? Yes it did; however, there is still something wrong.

TRUTH

As we've already quoted, Jesus said: *"You shall know the truth, and the truth shall make you free"* (Jn. 8:32). He didn't say that we would have manifestations, etc., and that would set us free, but rather that we would *"know the truth."*

The reason these good Christians find that their problems are still with them, despite the fact that God greatly moved upon them, is because they don't know the truth.

Listen again to what Jesus said: *"The Spirit of the Lord is upon Me, because He has anointed Me to ... preach deliverance to the captives"* (Lk. 4:18).

If it is to be noticed, He didn't say that we are to *deliver* the captives, but rather *"preach deliverance to the captives,"* which is exactly what I'm doing to you in this book.

The term, *preach deliverance*, means to explain what deliverance is, which refers to being delivered from the domain of darkness to the domain of light, and how it is obtained. The latter comes exclusively by our faith in Christ and what Christ has done for us at the Cross. The Cross is where the believer's victory is, and it is where the believer's victory remains. There is only one sacrifice for sin, not 10, not five, not even two, only one (Heb. 10:12). That sacrifice is the Cross. So, when we speak of going beyond the Cross, in short, we blaspheme. There is nothing beyond the Cross because there needs to be nothing beyond the Cross in that the Cross answered all questions and provided all solutions. That's the reason that Paul referred to the sacrifice of Christ as *"the everlasting covenant"* (Heb. 13:20).

OPPRESSION

"Now therefore, behold, the cry of the children of Israel is come unto Me: and I have also seen the oppression wherewith the Egyptians oppress them" (Ex. 3:9).

The Lord knew the sorrows of His people, He heard their cries, and He saw their oppression. Matthew Henry said:

"As the poorest of the oppressed are not below God's cognizance, so the highest and greatest of their oppressors are not above His check, but He will surely visit for these things."

Oppression comes from Satan. It is lethal, and its deliverance can only be effected by the power of God. The world of psychology, psychotherapy, psychological counseling, drugs, etc., can only worsen the oppressed. There is no help from these sources. Egypt cannot and, of course, will not deliver from Egypt.

GOD'S TIMING

God is now ready to accomplish His promise made to Abraham and repeated to Isaac and Jacob. He had not come down to see if, indeed, the subjects of His promise were in such a condition as to merit His salvation: it was sufficient for Him that they needed it. Their oppressed state, their sorrows, their tears, their sighs, and their heavy bondage had all come in review before Him. Blessed be His name; He counts His people's sighs and puts their tears into His bottle.

When God does a thing is just as important as *what* He does. Actually, it wouldn't be in the best interest of all for God to do certain things until the right time has come. That has to do with the condition of the person. As we've already stated, Israel would not have desired to leave Egypt if they had continued to be treated in a positive manner as they had been treated under Joseph. Before God's will can be brought about in our lives, we have to come to the place that we want that which will be brought about. Most often, circumstances have to be brought about for us to come to this frame of mind. Men do not normally do anything, even obey God, until they think it's in their best interest to do so; consequently, the Lord has to bring circumstances about until man sees that it is now in his best interest. As long as he is getting by fairly well in the state he's in, no matter how wrong that state might be, he is not apt to change. So, the Lord has to allow oppression to come about in order for us to see where we are and how that we desperately need to change.

THE CROSS

Bringing all of this up to the present time, for that which happened to the children of Israel is definitely a type of all that happens to us as believers, there are some things we need to know.

The slain lamb, in effect, was that which would deliver Israel and was, of course, a type of Christ. As the Lord would bring them to the slain lamb, likewise, most all, if not all of God's dealings with us, is to bring us to the foot of the Cross. The Cross is the answer for all depression, oppression, suppression, emotional disturbances, fear, anxiety, worry, etc.

The word *oppression* in the Hebrew is *lachats* and means *"distress, affliction, to crush, force, hold fast, or to press."*

Oppression is one of Satan's greatest hindrances as it relates to the child of God. Probably, a spirit of depression is the culminating result of oppression, etc. As stated, the answer to that, and, in fact, the only answer, is the Cross.

HOW IS THE CROSS THE ANSWER TO OPPRESSION?

Oppression comes from without, the powers of darkness, and depression comes from both without and within. The latter, as well, is the power of darkness that has come upon an individual and is that which one cannot dismiss by his own power.

Some have stated that depression is actually a concentrated, overbearing interest in oneself. It is probably the highest form of selfishness and is an ego gone awry. However, the person so afflicted does not at all see it that way; nevertheless, it is believed by some that is the problem.

I suspect there is at least some truth in this statement.

Probably, if we were able to get to the root of the problem of depression, oppression, etc., we would find in any case and in every circumstance that self is really the major problem with the human being. That's the reason that the foolishness of the self-esteem theory has made such headway in the last several decades. In that false direction, the idea is, if one's self-esteem can be built up, then one's problems will be solved. While it is certainly true that one can have a low self-esteem or a high self-esteem, the problem is still self. The Bible lends no credence whatsoever to this theory of self-esteem.

The cure for this problem, and I might quickly add, the only cure, is the Cross of Christ. The believer is to understand that every single thing we receive from God is made possible by the Cross of Christ. As we have repeatedly stated, if we will place our faith exclusively in Christ, and exclusively in what He did for us at the Cross, the Holy Spirit will then go to work within our hearts and lives, doing what only He can do. That is the solution, and it is the only solution.

At the Cross, Jesus defeated every single power of darkness (Col. 2:10-15). He did so by atoning for all sin — past, present, and future — at least for those who will believe (Jn. 3:16). To be sure, the work was so complete at the Cross that no part of it will ever have to be repeated.

Peter said: *"Grace and peace be multiplied unto you through the knowledge of God, and of Jesus our Lord* (this is both sanctifying grace and sanctifying peace, all made available by the Cross),

"According as His divine power has given unto us all things (the Lord with large-handed generosity has given us all things) *that pertain unto life and godliness* (pertains to the fact that the Lord Jesus has given us everything we need regarding life and living), *through the knowledge of Him who has called us to glory and virtue* (the *knowledge* addressed here speaks of what Christ did at the Cross, which alone can provide *glory* and *virtue*):

"Whereby are given unto us exceeding great and precious promises (pertains to the Word of God, which alone holds the answer to every life problem): *that by these* (promises) *you might be partakers of the divine nature* (the divine nature implanted in the inner being of the believing sinner

becomes the source of our new life and actions; it comes to everyone at the moment of being born again), *having escaped the corruption that is in the world through lust.* (This presents the salvation experience of the sinner and the sanctification experience of the saint)" (II Pet. 1:2-4).

THE CAUSE

When the believing sinner comes to Christ, as stated, at that moment, he is placed *"in Christ,"* which means that he is beyond oppression, etc. (Jn. 14:20). So, why is it that many Christians continue to have great difficulties in this capacity?

The cause with this is the same thing as the cause with anything else as it regards the believer. Not knowing or understanding the Cross as it regards sanctification, as one must understand the Cross, the believer allows his faith to be moved to other things. In other words, the Cross ceases to be the object of his faith, with it then being placed in something else. Please believe me, there are myriad preachers trying to pull your faith to things and places which will not only be worthless to you, but will actually cause problems instead of solving problems.

The believer must place his faith in the Cross, understanding that it is through the Cross that he receives all benefits from the Lord, and I mean all. As well, he must keep his faith in the Cross, not allowing it to be moved to other things. When this is done, the Holy Spirit will then guarantee all the benefits of the Cross, in effect, what Jesus there did (Rom. 6:1–14; 8:1–11; I Cor. 1:17–18, 23; 2:2; Col. 2:10-15).

That which I have just given you is the only way to walk in victory, and that means victory in every capacity, including oppression, depression, nervous disorders, fear, anxiety, etc. The Lord alone is the Deliverer, but He always, and without exception, delivers by the means of the finished work of Christ, all carried out by the Holy Spirit.

IS THE CHURCH TAUGHT THIS FOUNDATIONAL TRUTH?

Regrettably, it is not!

The Cross was strongly taught in the 1800s and perhaps in the early 1900s, but in the last several decades, the church has been pulled away from the Cross to other things. While there have been many contributing factors toward this, perhaps the worst influence of all has been the so-called Word of Faith doctrine. In fact, that doctrine has been very predominant in the modern church for the last several decades, especially among Pentecostals and Charismatics.

In that particular teaching, it is taught that the believer should have nothing to do with the Cross. The Cross was and is referred to in those circles as *"past miseries."* The Cross has been deemed *"as the greatest defeat in human history."* In fact, in many Word of Faith churches, no songs are to be sung about the Cross, the blood, etc.

This doctrine may mention the blood of Christ in a positive way at times, but it actually teaches that salvation comes not by the Cross, but rather by Jesus going to hell as a sinner.

They teach that He suffered three days and nights in hell, and we speak of the burning side of hell, where He was tormented by demons. At the conclusion of the three days and nights, God then said, *"It is enough."* Jesus was then born again and raised from the dead. So, in effect, they teach that salvation comes by the means of this fictitious story, because this which I have just stated is not found anywhere in the Bible. It is pure fiction!

THE JESUS DIED SPIRITUALLY DOCTRINE

Some may claim that what we're discussing is nothing more than semantics. In other words, it's the same thing that all other preachers preach and teach, but worded in a little different way.

No, it's not the same thing. The Jesus Died Spiritually doctrine, for that's what it is, is an attack upon the atonement and, in fact, the greatest attack, more than likely, in human history. Those who practice and proclaim this teaching can only be described as *"enemies of the Cross of Christ."*

Of these people, Paul said: *"For many walk, of whom I have told you often, and now tell you even weeping, that they are the enemies of the Cross of Christ:*

"Whose end is destruction, whose god is their belly, and whose glory is in their shame, who mind earthly things" (Phil. 3:18–19).

While there are certainly many other attacks against the Cross, this which I have mentioned is, I believe, the most lethal and deadly of them all. A sinner cannot be saved by believing the Word of Faith doctrine; hence, very little attempt is even made to get people saved in those circles. While some few may be saved in those particular meetings, etc., to be sure, they aren't saved by believing that particular doctrine, but by simply trusting Christ. However, the truth is, the number of salvations in that sector is small indeed! In fact, their teachers claim that their business is not to get people saved, but rather to enlighten them after they are saved. As well, there are precious few people baptized with the Holy Spirit in those circles, precious few delivered by the power of God, and precious few healed. In fact, according to that doctrine, which is totally erroneous, no one, as stated, is saved, delivered, healed, etc. So, what is the great attraction of this particular form of doctrine?

MONEY

The great attraction is greed. The basic thrust of this doctrine is money. In other words, its gurus claim that if one follows their teachings, one will get rich. There seems to be enough greed in all of us to make such a doctrine very enticing.

Let me again quote Paul when he said, *"Whose god is their belly, and whose glory is in their shame, who mind earthly things."* This describes that doctrine to the proverbial T.

So the church has been pulled away from the Cross, not only in the realm of which I speak, but in another as well.

HUMANISTIC PSYCHOLOGY

Almost every major denomination, and perhaps all major denominations, promote humanistic psychology as the answer to the ills of man. To be sure, these denominations do not take a neutral position regarding this of which we speak, but rather promote the world of psychology, and do so on an extended basis. While many of these so-called preachers and religious leaders would claim to believe in the Cross, the truth is, one cannot promote both causes at the same time. Jesus said: *"No servant can serve two masters: for either he will hate the one, and love the other; or else he will hold to the one, and despise the other. You cannot serve God and mammon"* (Lk. 16:13).

Psychology is not a viable science, and no true scientist will claim that it is. In fact, there is no proof that it's ever helped anyone. The truth is, psychology is the answer of humanism to the Bible.

We claim that the Bible holds the answer for every spiritual and emotional problem that man might have. We claim there is no other answer except that which is given in the Word of God.

A vote for humanistic psychology is, at the same time, a vote of no confidence as it regards the Cross.

So, through these twin evils of humanistic psychology and the Word of Faith doctrine, which, in reality, is no faith at all, at least that which God will honor, Satan has made great inroads in the church as it regards a denial of the Cross.

Let me remind the reader that the only One who could deliver the children of Israel out of Egyptian bondage was the Lord. At the same time, He is still the only One who can deliver.

OUT OF EGYPT

"Come now therefore, and I will send you unto Pharaoh, that you may bring forth My people the children of Israel out of Egypt" (Ex. 3:10).

As the Lord used Moses as His instrument, He continues to use the fivefold calling of apostles, prophets, evangelists, pastors, and teachers (Eph. 4:11). Even though man is the instrument, it is God who delivers.

Due to the fivefold calling functioning under the new covenant, the manner in which God uses such instruments is a little different now than it was under the old covenant. The principle, one might say, is the same, but the manner is somewhat different.

Under the old covenant, things which were carried out by the prophets were mostly done by that which one would refer to as raw, naked power. Presently, and we should say since the Cross, it is now done by teaching. Jesus said, *"The Spirit of the Lord is upon Me, because He has anointed me to ... preach deliverance to the captives"* (Lk. 4:18).

In fact, as I've previously stated, this is exactly what we're doing in this book, *"preaching deliverance to the captives."*

As well, the Lord had to bring His people out of Egypt. There was no way they could remain in Egypt and continue to be the people of God. It is the same presently.

SEPARATION AND ISOLATION

The Lord must bring His people presently out of the system of this world. While we're *in* the world, we are to never be *of* the world. That's the business of the Holy Spirit as He constantly seeks to separate us from the world.

However, while separation is definitely that which the Holy Spirit demands, it is not isolation. In fact, as *"lights,"* we as believers are to illuminate this world. As *"salt,"* we are to preserve that which is right and righteous. That's why Jesus also said, *"You are the salt of the earth ... you are the light of the world. A city that is set on an hill cannot be hid"* (Mat. 5:13–14).

In fact, the only light in this world, and we speak of spiritual light, is that provided by the child of God, who, in reality, is a reflection of Christ. The only thing that keeps it from being destroyed, i.e., salt, is the righteousness of the believer.

WHO AM I?

"And Moses said unto God, Who am I, that I should go unto Pharaoh, and that I should bring forth the children of Israel out of Egypt?" (Ex. 3:11).

The carnal mind is not subject to the law of God, neither indeed can be. The very Moses, who in Chapter 2:11–13 stepped forward with energy to champion his people, is the very same Moses, who in Chapter 3:11–13 stepped back and declared himself unequal to the enterprise. True faith neither steps forward nor backward but holds His hand who says, *"Certainly I will be with you."*

The glorious name *I AM*, i.e., *Jehovah*, was now first made known to Israel. To Abraham, to Isaac, and to Jacob, He revealed Himself as *El Shaddai*, that is, *"God, the Almighty,"* for that was the revelation they needed. However, to Israel, enslaved and helpless, a further revelation was necessary, and so the glorious name I AM was given to her as a blank check so that she could write after these two words whatever her need demanded.

If Israel needed a deliverer, at once, she had the answer, *"I AM the Deliverer."* She needed a comforter and again came the response, *"I AM the Comforter."* She needed all kinds of provision — needs immeasurably beyond human skill to meet — and, at once, her faithful God said, *"I AM the Provider."*

MOSES

Moses shrank back at what God proposed. He, just one man, was going to be sent to Pharaoh, the mightiest monarch at that time on the face of the earth, and the leader of the most powerful nation on earth. By this one man, the children of Israel were going to be led out of Egypt. His answer to this monumental task, in fact, the greatest task ever proposed for one man, was, *"Who am I?"*

God never asks of us something that we can do. He always asks of us that which is impossible for us to do. In fact, if we can do it, then there's no point in God becoming involved.

This means that every single calling placed upon an individual, irrespective of what that calling might be, is far and away beyond the ability of that person to carry it out. It is designed that way for purpose and reason.

As stated, the Lord uses human instrumentation, but it must be human instrumentation which realizes that it cannot accomplish the task unless the Lord gives the power to do so.

Now, while we should know and understand that we within ourselves cannot do this thing, at the same time, we must also understand that with God, we can get the job done. As stated, faith never moves forward or backward. It holds the hand of the One who is doing the leading, namely the Lord.

I AM IS TO BE LINKED TO I

In fact, when God began to tell Moses what to do, the die had already been cast. In other words, God had come down to deliver the children of Israel, and the combined power of earth and hell could not hold them in captivity one hour beyond His appointed time.

When Moses went forward in the energy of the flesh (Ex. 2:11), he was full of confidence in the success of his mission. This comes out clearly in Acts 7:25: *"For he supposed his brethren would have understood how that God by His hand would deliver them: but they understood not."* However, now that the call of God had definitely come to him for this work, and, as well, it was God's time, he was very conscious of the difficulties in the way. The discipline of the backside of the desert had not been in vain. Shepherding had chastened him.

We preachers are quick to chasten Moses for his retiring attitude. We label it as a lack of faith, etc. However, I would ask the question: Were such a command given by God to any of us presently, would our response be any different, or even as good?

As is obvious, the Lord didn't mince words, but what He was demanding of this man was so absolutely astounding that it defied all description. So, in the face of such a task, the question, *"Who am I?"* seems to be appropriate. However, as Moses is now to see, I AM is to be linked to *"I."*

FAITH

"And He said, Certainly I will be with you; and this shall be a token unto you, that I have sent you: When you have brought forth the people out of Egypt, you shall serve God upon this mountain" (Ex. 3:12).

"Certainly I will be with you," should have been translated, *"Since I will be with you,"* because that's what it actually and literally says in the Hebrew. In other words, there is no doubt about the presence of God being with Moses, that a guaranteed fact.

Moses was excusing himself on the grounds of insufficiency, but God replied, *"I will supply that which you lack. I will impart all the qualities you need."*

Then He said to Moses that not only would he succeed in leading the children of Israel out of Egyptian bondage, but they would then worship on this very mountain, which evidently was Sinai, where, a short time later, the Ten Commandments and the law would be given.

As well, as the Lord promised to be with Moses, He promises to be with every single believer whom He calls for a certain task. As Moses had the promise of God, we, as well, have the promise of God. Consequently, we should not look at the task before us, but rather at the God of Glory who is going to help us to perform the task, always realizing that there is nothing He cannot do. However, we must make certain that God has called us, and we haven't called ourselves.

WHAT SHALL I SAY UNTO THEM?

"And Moses said unto God, Behold, when I come unto the children of Israel, and shall say unto them, The God of your fathers has sent me unto you; and they shall say to me, What is His name? what shall I say unto them?" (Ex. 3:13).

The human heart is full of questions; consequently, it reasons and questions when unhesitating obedience is that which is due to God. Still more marvelous is the grace that bears with all the reasonings and answers all the questions. Each question, in fact, seems to elicit some new feature of divine grace.

To the Israelites, God had been known only by titles, such as *El* or *Elohim,* meaning *"the Lofty One";* or *Shaddai,* which means *"the Powerful";* or *Jahveh* or *Jehovah,* the *"Existent One."*

These titles were used among the Israelites with some perception of their meaning, but yet, these names were more descriptions than anything else.

As well, the Egyptians used the word *god* generically and had a special name for each particular god such as *Ammon, Phthah, Ra, Mentu,* etc. Knowing that the Egyptians set much store by the names of their gods, which in every case had a meaning, Moses reasoned that Israel would want to know the name of God who had sent him. As we shall see, Israel came to cherish the name that God told Moses to use as it regarded the deity.

THE DIVINELY SENT DELIVERER

Let us not be too quick to condemn Moses here — the Lord did not! This was no small difficulty for Moses. No visible presence would accompany him. He was to go alone to the enslaved Hebrews and present himself as the divinely-sent deliverer. He was to tell them that the God of their fathers had promised to free them. But, as we shall see later, this was not likely to make much impression upon a people who were, at least for the most part, sunk in the idolatries of the Egyptians. So, the great lawgiver-to-be felt that they would quickly want to know: *"Who is this God?*

What is His character? Prove to us that He is worthy of our confidence."

Concerning this, Pink says: *"And does not a similar difficulty arise before us! We go forth to tell lost sinners of a God they have never seen. In His name we bid them trust. But cannot we anticipate the response — 'Show us the Father, and it suffices us' is still, in substance, the demand of the doubting heart. Moses felt this difficulty; and so do we."*

I AM THAT I AM

"And God said unto Moses, I AM THAT I AM: and He said, Thus shall you say unto the children of Israel, I AM has sent me unto you" (Ex. 3:14).

It is said that the quotation, *"I AM THAT I AM,"* is the best translation that can be given of the Hebrew words. Some have translated it, *"I will be that I will be,"* and others, *"I am because I am"*; however, I AM THAT I AM says it better.

This name was cherished by the Jews as a sacred treasure and recognized as the proper appellation of the one and only God whom the Israelites worshiped. It is found in this sense on the Moabite stone, in the fragments of Philo-Byblius, and elsewhere.

The idea expressed by the name, I AM THAT I AM, is that expressed of a *"real, perfect, unconditioned, independent existence."*

Dr. Pentecost translated the name (if we would call it that) I AM THAT I AM, as, *"I was, I am, and I shall always continue to be."*

Pink says, "*The principle contained in this word of Jehovah to Moses contains timely instruction for us. We are to go forth declaring the name and nature of God as He has been revealed. No attempts are to be made to prove His existence; no time should be wasted with men in efforts to reason about God. Our business is to proclaim the being of God as He has revealed Himself in and through Jesus Christ. The 'I AM' of the burning bush now stands fully declared in the blessed person of our Saviour who said, 'I am the Bread of Life', 'I am the Good Shepherd', 'I am the Door', 'I am the Light of the World', 'I am the Way, the Truth, and the Life', 'I am the Resurrection and the Life', 'I am the True Vine'. He is the eternal 'I AM' — 'the same yesterday, and today, and forever.'*"

In the name or appellative, I AM THAT I AM, we have a depth which no finite mind can fathom. It means that God is self-existent, beside whom there is none else. He is without beginning and without ending; "*from everlasting to everlasting,*" He is God. None but He can say, "*I AM THAT I AM*" — always the same, eternally changeless.

THE TITLE

The title that God gives Himself here is one of great significance. When we look at the various names which God has given Himself, we see that these names are connected with the particular needs of the people.

For instance:

Jehovah-Jireh means, *"the Lord will provide."*
Jehovah-Nissi means, *"the Lord my banner."*
Jehovah-Shalom means, *"the Lord is my peace."*
Jehovah-Tsidkenu means, *"the Lord our righteousness."*

Of course, there are many other such like titles that we could give.

However, all of these titles are unfolded to meet the necessities of His people. When He calls Himself *"I AM,"* it comprehends every title. In effect, in taking this title, the Lord was furnishing His people with a blank check to be filled up to any amount. He calls Himself *"I AM,"* and faith has but to write over against that precious name whatever we want. God is the only significant figure, and human need may add the ciphers. If we want life, Christ says, *"I AM the life"*; if we want righteousness, He is *"the Lord our righteousness"*; if we want peace, *"He is our peace,"* etc.

THE PRESENT MEANING

As we've already stated, the revelation of God to man has taken on many appearances. However, all of these revelations have led up to the great revelation, in fact, the greatest of them all and, in actuality, the final revelation. We speak of God revealing Himself in Jesus Christ. When Philip asked our Lord to show him and the other disciples the Father, Jesus answered: *"Have I been so long with you, and yet have you not known Me, Philip? He who has seen Me has seen the Father"* (Jn. 14:8-9).

When Jesus gave all of His followers the right to use His name (Mk. 16:17), He was, in effect, saying the same thing that God said to Moses, *"I AM THAT I AM."*

The blank check holds true as much presently as it did then, but it must be looked at in the following way: The Lord will never allow His name or His Word to be used against Himself, in other words, to bring about that which is not His will. Such a disposition would be none other than catastrophic.

It is the business of the believer to ascertain the will of God, which can definitely be done if the person will consecrate to the Lord. Then, in the context of the will of God, the blank check holds, but only in that context.

GOD IS A BIG GOD, SO ASK BIG

However, in that context, and incidentally, that is the context which is correct and right, great and mighty things can be done, and, in fact, great and might things have been done. My grandmother used to tell me and, in fact, told me many times and in many and varied ways, *"Jimmy, God is a big God, so ask big."* I have never forgotten that advice, and it has helped me to touch this world for the Lord Jesus Christ. God is big, so we should ask big.

Moses was to tell the children of Israel, *"I AM has sent me unto you."* There could be no higher authority than that. To be sure, it would be proven by the miracles that would follow.

At this present time, we have all types of preachers claiming all types of things, and doing so in the name of the Lord, when, in reality, the Lord has not sent them. How do we know that?

When precious few people are saved, if any; when precious few are baptized with the Holy Spirit, if any; when precious few are delivered, if any; and when precious few are truly healed, if any, that is a telltale sign that something is wrong. That is the state of most of the modern church.

As it regards most evangelists, while the crowds may be large, and the accolades may flow thickly and freely, when the dust settles and the smoke clears, one finds very little that's truly being done for Christ. It's mostly all fluff.

FALSE PROPHETS

Just last night, a dear lady was in our service at Family Worship Center and related to me how a particular evangelist, who is well known, claimed to be speaking prophetically and told her that she would live to be 100 years of age.

To cut straight through to the bottom line, this man is a false prophet, and I'm not so sure that the dear lady didn't shorten her life by seeking the help of this false prophet. Great and glowing statements made by these individuals, who claim to be of God and from God, most of the time turn out to be the opposite. In other words, the patient who is declared to be healed suddenly dies.

The point I'm making is, I'm concerned that in many of these cases, these false pronouncements by these false prophets actually put a curse upon the people instead of a blessing.

But yet, the far greater majority of the modern church goes on its merry way, and few question these false pronouncements, irrespective as to how off-base they actually are, and how much they prove to be empty, hollow, and worthless. Satan is a master at getting people to believe that what is of God isn't, and what isn't of God is!

But yet, in all of it, there are still a few men and women of God who truly are called of God and are truly being used by God. Though they be few, thank God for the few!

THE GOD OF ABRAHAM, THE GOD OF ISAAC, AND THE GOD OF JACOB

"And God said moreover unto Moses, Thus shall you say unto the children of Israel, The LORD God of your fathers, the God of Abraham, the God of Isaac, and the God of Jacob, has sent me unto you: this is My name forever, and this is My memorial unto all generations.

"Go, and gather the elders of Israel together, and say unto them, The LORD God of your fathers, the God of Abraham, of Isaac, and of Jacob, appeared unto me, saying, I

have surely visited you, and seen that which is done to you in Egypt" (Ex. 3:15-16).

Moses was commanded to tell the children of Israel that this mighty God, Jehovah, was the God of Abraham, the God of Isaac, and the God of Jacob. This is His name forever and His memorial to all generations.

He changes not; He is the same yesterday, today, and forever. His name is Jesus, and that is God's greatest name!

The glad tidings of great joy that Moses was to carry to Israel were these: *"I will bring you up out of the affliction of Egypt into a land flowing with milk and honey."* This was the message, and Moses' faith in delivering it was strengthened beforehand by the divine assurance that it would be believed.

As we come to it, the three days' journey of Verse 18 was not deceitfully proposed by God, but furnished as a test for Pharaoh.

THE WORD OF THE LORD TO MOSES

As is understood, the Lord was telling Moses these things while he was still at the backside of the desert. In essence, the Lord told him several things that would happen:

- Upon arriving in Egypt, Moses was to gather the elders of Israel before him, which pertained to the leaders of the enslaved tribes. Perhaps, these were the heads of the tribes.

- He was to tell them that *"The LORD God of your fathers, the God of Abraham, the God of Isaac, and the God of Jacob, has sent me unto you."*
- The name of God was to be I AM THAT I AM, which was a new revelation to Israel.
- Moses was to tell the Israelites that God had seen and, in fact, continued to see all the evil that was being done to them in Egypt.
- God had said that He would bring them out of the affliction of Egypt unto the land of the Canaanites, etc.
- It was a land flowing with milk and honey.
- Whereas some 40 years before, the leaders of Israel had not hearkened unto Moses, this time, the Lord remonstrated, they definitely would hearken to the voice of Moses, for evidently, the Lord would prepare the way.
- Moses and the elders of Israel, along with Aaron, the brother of Moses, it would later prove, were to appear before Pharaoh.
- They were to demand of Pharaoh that he let Israel go for a three days' journey into the wilderness that they might sacrifice there to the Lord their God.
- The Lord foretold that Pharaoh would not heed their demand, and then God said that He would smite Egypt with all miracles and wonders.
- After that, Pharaoh would definitely let the people go.
- When the Israelites would leave Egypt, they would not leave empty but would be loaded down with silver, gold, and raiment, which the Egyptians would give them.

So, in a few words, the Lord told Moses exactly what was to happen, therefore, what he could expect.

A WITNESS

The phrase, *"I have surely visited you, and seen that which is done to you in Egypt,"* proclaims the fact that the Lord is not unmindful of anything that happens to His children. Sometimes it may seem as if He is not observing that which is happening, but He most definitely is. To be sure, exactly as we see what happened to Egypt, the Lord is going to require of the offender every iota of that which has been practiced on the offended. That's the reason He told us not to avenge ourselves, *"but rather give place unto wrath: for it is written, Vengeance is Mine; I will repay, saith the Lord"* (Rom. 12:19).

We are to place all wrongs, all injustices, and all hurts tendered toward us and upon us into the hand of the Lord. We are to forgive the people, whomever they might be, ask the Lord to help us forget about the situation, and proceed on with our lives and living for the Lord, leaving all in His hands.

To be sure, God never forgets, unless its sins of which we repent.

BEFORE PHARAOH

"And I have said, I will bring you up out of the affliction of Egypt unto the land of the Canaanites, and the Hittites,

and the Amorites, and the Perizzites, and the Hivites, and the Jebusites, unto a land flowing with milk and honey.

"And they shall hearken to your voice: and you shall come, you and the elders of Israel, unto the king of Egypt, and you shall say unto him, The LORD *God of the Hebrews has met with us: and now let us go, we beseech you, three days' journey into the wilderness, that we may sacrifice to the* LORD *our God"* (Ex. 3:17-18).

The glad tidings of great joy that Moses was to carry to Israel were these: *"I will bring you up out of the affliction of Egypt into a land flowing with milk and honey."* This was the message, and Moses' faith in delivering it was strengthened beforehand by the divine assurance that it would be believed.

By the Lord telling Moses that the elders of Israel would definitely believe his message, it tells us that Moses had expressed fear that they wouldn't.

The idea is, the hearts of men are in God's hands, and He is able to bring about that which He desires without infringing upon the free moral agency of anyone.

GOD IS UNLIMITED

This is at least one of the reasons that we should look to the Lord for leading in all things. We as believers should never trust in our own personal wisdom, acumen, ability, or strength. Our knowledge of situations is very limited, while God's knowledge is unlimited. Our ability, as well, is very limited, while the ability of God is unlimited. We should trust Him and ardently seek His face about everything we do, whether it is small or great.

It is easy to see here that God already had things planned out and, through foreknowledge, knew exactly what would happen. All Moses had to do was to follow the leading of the Lord, which he definitely did. It is the same with us presently because God cannot change, and He doesn't need to change.

He has things on our behalf already planned out, and that which He has planned will definitely be accomplished, that is, if we cooperate with Him, thereby, walking in faith. However, remember, there must be cooperation on our part, and that cooperation is summed up in one word, *faith*.

WHAT DO WE MEAN BY FAITH?

God is not looking for perfection in people because, sadly and regrettably, there isn't any perfection, but He definitely is looking for faith. He wants us to believe Him. If we will believe Him, thereby, having our faith in the correct object, despite our shortcomings, He can see us through.

As we shall see, the children of Israel were to place their faith in God, which would ultimately carry out to faith in the slain lamb, which, in effect, would bring about their deliverance from Egypt. It was the Cross then, of which the slain lamb was a type (the Passover lamb), and it is the Cross now. If our faith is placed there, understanding that the great plan of God in its totality is centered up in the Cross, making the Cross the centrality of the gospel, victory will most definitely be ours.

It was a part of God's design that sacrifice, which was interrupted for various reasons during the sojourn in Egypt, should be resumed beyond the bounds of Egypt by His people. Consequently, it was *sacrifice* that was first mentioned to Pharaoh, regarding the first visit by Moses to that monarch.

Demanding that the Israelites be allowed to go three days' journey into the wilderness in order that they may sacrifice unto the Lord was not meant to deceive Pharaoh, but rather to test him.

Going back to Verse 15, the Lord told Moses to tell the children of Israel that *"the LORD God of your fathers, the God of Abraham, the God of Isaac, and the God of Jacob, has sent me unto you: this is My name forever, and this is My memorial unto all generations."*

THE TRUTH

This statement contains a very important truth — a truth which many professing Christians seem to forget, namely, that God's relationship with Israel is an eternal one. He is just as much Israel's God now as when He visited them in the land of Egypt. Only because of rejecting their Messiah, they are, in His governmental dealings, set aside for a time. However, His Word is clear and emphatic: *"This is My name forever."* He does not say, *"This is My name for a time, so long as they continue what they ought to be."* No, *"This is My name forever, and this is My memorial unto all generations."*

When Paul said, *"God has not cast away His people which He foreknew"* (Rom. 11:2), this meant they were His people still—whether obedient or disobedient, united together or scattered abroad, or manifested to the nations or hidden from their view. Whether they like it or not, they are His people, and He is their God.

This doesn't mean that all of them are saved. In fact, precious few of them presently are saved; consequently, those in that state, which includes almost all, have died, and will die, eternally lost. However, it does mean that the promises of God, as it regards the nation and these people as a whole, will definitely be realized. Exodus 3:15 is unanswerable.

HAS GOD SURRENDERED THE LOT OF HIS INHERITANCE?

God means what He says, and He will ere long make manifest to all the nations of the earth that His connection with Israel is one which shall outlive all the revolutions of time. *"The gifts and calling of God are without repentance."* When He said, *"This is My name forever,"* He spoke absolutely. I AM declared Himself to be Israel's God forever. All the Gentiles shall be made to bow to this and to know, moreover, that all God's providential dealings with them in all their destinies are connected, in some way or other, with that favored and honored, though now judged and scattered, people.

"When the Most High divided to the nations their inheritance, when He separated the sons of Adam, He set

the bounds of the people according to the number of the children of Israel. For the LORD's portion is His people; Jacob is the lot of His inheritance" (Deut. 32:8–9).

Mackintosh asked this question: *"Has this ceased to be true? Has Jehovah given up His 'portion,' and surrendered 'the lot of His inheritance'?"*

To reply to these questions would be to quote a large portion of the Old Testament and not a little of the New Testament. In answer, we must say, let not Christendom *"be ignorant of this mystery ... that blindness in part is happened to Israel, until the fullness of the Gentiles be come in. And so all Israel shall be saved"* (Rom. 11:25–26).

THE SACRIFICE

To which we've already briefly alluded, the first thing that Moses was to mention to Pharaoh was the fact of the sacrifice and its necessity.

The sacrifice of an innocent victim — either a lamb, a goat, a heifer, an ox, or a ram — was instituted upon the fall of the first family. Every evidence is that God told Adam and Eve how fellowship could be restored and sins forgiven, which would be by virtue of the sacrifice, and more particularly, what it represented, namely, the coming Christ. A perfect description of this is given in Genesis, Chapter 4, as it regards Cain and Abel. Abel offered up the sacrifice that was pleasing to God. It was an innocent victim, which typified Christ. With the sacrifice being accepted, the sacrificer was accepted as well. God didn't really look at the one offering the sacrifice, but rather He looked at the sacrifice. He continues to do the same presently. Likewise, if the sacrifice was rejected, even as it was with Cain, then the sacrificer was rejected also.

Thereafter until Moses, a period of about 2,400 years, the patriarch of each family was to serve as the priest of that family and superintend the offering up of sacrifices, which, in fact, were continued throughout that period of time.

After the deliverance of the children of Israel from Egyptian bondage, which we are now in the process of studying, the Lord gave to Moses and the children of Israel His law, which covered every aspect of their daily lives and living. The center or core of the law was the sacrificial system. It was carried out in elaborate detail and was meant to symbolize Christ, as, in fact, all sacrifices were meant to symbolize Christ (see our book, *The Sacrificial System*).

A STOPGAP MEASURE

In fact, the blood of bulls and goats was merely a stopgap measure, which was to be used until Christ would come, and would ever point to Him. Animal blood could never take away sin, but the spotless, pure, unsullied blood of the Lord Jesus Christ definitely could take away sin and, in fact, did atone for all sin, in it being shed (Eph. 2:13–18; I Pet. 1:18–20).

When Christ came, animal sacrifices were no more needed, as would be obvious, because Christ had fulfilled that symbol. Unfortunately, the Christian Jews, and we especially speak of those in Jerusalem, continued to try to meld the sacrifice of Christ with the ancient sacrificial system, as carried out at the temple. As I think the historical narrative records, this was not pleasing to the Lord. So, in A.D. 70, the Lord used as His instrument the Roman general Titus, who headed up the mighty Tenth Legion, to destroy Jerusalem and, above all, the temple. It was so completely destroyed that there was nothing left, with even a harrow being dragged over the spot where it had once stood.

In effect, the Lord was saying that Christ must no longer be insulted by animal sacrifices continuing to be offered, so He removed the means and the manner of those sacrifices.

THE GOVERNMENT OF GRACE

Unfortunately, some in the modern church are attempting to go back into the law of Moses and to try to keep the feast days, the Sabbath, etc. Such would have to be construed by the Lord as an abomination. These people doing this are saying, whether they realize it or not, that what Christ did at the Cross was insufficient, and so other things must be added. The moment we do that, we fall from grace (Gal. 5:4).

I have noticed some preachers and others attempting to wear Jewish prayer shawls, which can be labeled as none other than sin. The reason that it's sin is because Paul said, *"For whatsoever is not of faith is sin"* (Rom. 14:23). Anything that abrogates the sacrifice of Christ insults Christ, and that no sane person wants to do.

We are living now under the government of grace. There is only one way that one can function under the government of grace, and that is by and through faith, and we speak of faith in Christ and His finished work (I Cor. 1:17–18, 21, 23; 2:2, 5).

Some Christians erroneously believe that because this is the dispensation of grace, and it definitely is that, then we're automatically functioning in grace. No, we aren't!

Paul said, "*I do not frustrate the grace of God: for if righteousness come by the law, then Christ is dead in vain*" (Gal. 2:21).

This passage proves to us that it is possible to frustrate the grace of God. The word *frustrate* in the Greek is *atheteo* and means, "*to set aside, to neutralize or violate, bring to naught.*"

So, we know from this statement that it definitely is possible to stop the flow of the grace of God into our lives, which brings on untold problems. The only way we can function as Christians is by a steady, uninterrupted flow of the grace of God, which simply means that the goodness of God is extended to undeserving believers.

THE CROSS OF CHRIST

The grace of God, which constitutes the government of grace, functions on the principle of the Cross of Christ, and through no other means. In fact, God has no more grace today than He had thousands of years ago. Due to the fact that the blood of bulls and goats couldn't take away sin, this hindered the full flow of the grace of God from coming to believers.

Upon the advent of the Cross, which removed the terrible sin debt (Jn. 1:29), the grace of God could now flow copiously to all believers. In order to have this uninterrupted flow, this abundant supply, the only thing that is required of the child of God is that we have faith in Christ and what Christ has done for us in His finished work of the Cross (I Cor. 1:17–18).

Continued faith in the sufferings of Christ guarantees a continued and uninterrupted flow of the grace of God. It is all dependent on the Cross. So, what did Paul mean by frustrating the grace of God?

THE FRUSTRATION OF THE GRACE OF GOD

Whenever the believer pulls his faith from Christ and the Cross, thereby, placing it in something else, in the mind of God, that believer has then gone from grace to law. Paul plainly said that if we can gain righteousness by the law or by keeping certain laws, then Christ died in vain. That's a pretty strong statement!

Whenever the Christian does this, and I speak of our faith being anchored in something other than the Cross, we are, in effect, saying, whether we realize it or not, that the work of Christ on the Cross was insufficient, and we need to add something to that particular work. Or else, we are saying that it was not the Cross that effected our redemption, but something else altogether. Either way, we are on the road to spiritual disaster.

LAW

When Paul mentioned law, he was either talking about the law of Moses or laws that we have devised ourselves — man-devised in some fashion. Actually, these laws, most of the time, are very good within themselves, and because they are very good, this fools us. It makes us believe that by the doing of such, such is the means of victory, overcoming power and strength, righteousness, holiness, Christlikeness, etc. However, the only thing we actually succeed in doing is to develop self-righteousness in our lives, which can cause us untold problems.

Our victory is solely in Christ and Christ alone. It is in Christ solely by virtue of what He did for us in the giving of Himself on the Cross. That's why the Apostle Paul said, *"But God forbid that I should glory* (boast), *save in the Cross of our Lord Jesus Christ, by whom the world is crucified unto me, and I unto the world"* (Gal. 6:14).

FOREKNOWLEDGE

"And I am sure that the king of Egypt will not let you go, no, not by a mighty hand" (Ex. 3:19).

Through foreknowledge, as recorded in Verse 19, God knew that Pharaoh would not allow the children of Israel to leave.

Consequently, as is portrayed in Verse 20, He would use Pharaoh's obstinate heart to serve as a warning of the power and glory of God to all the surrounding nations.

God can take whatever is done and turn it to His good if His people will only believe Him.

As we shall see, Verses 20 through 22 tell us that God planned that His people should receive proper wages for all their hard labor before leaving Egypt.

The word *borrow* in Verse 22 does not mean *"to borrow"* in the sense that we use the term. It means *"to ask"* or even *"to demand."*

The implication is that the Egyptians had stripped from the Israelites their valuables. Now, Israel would not only receive back what had been taken from them, but also what they had earned by their hard labor.

THE ABILITY OF GOD TO KNOW

Through foreknowledge, as stated, the Lord knew exactly what Pharaoh would do. In other words, through foreknowledge, God knows the future, which, of course, is beyond the comprehension of mere mortals.

However, when we speak of foreknowledge, we are not meaning that God predestines all things. While He definitely does predestine some things, all of these things which He does predestine are beyond the pale of man's free moral agency. In other words, God never tampers with the free moral agency of man, always respecting his free will.

As we survey the Scripture, we also find that everything that God predestines is in the realm of *what* will happen instead of *to whom* it will happen.

For instance, Paul said: *"For whom He did foreknow* (God knows who will accept Him as Lord and Saviour, even before we are born), *He also did predestinate to be conformed to the image of His Son, that He might be the firstborn among many brethren"* (Rom. 8:29).

The Scripture doesn't state here that a person is predestinated to be saved, while it definitely does say that God foreknows who will be saved. That is far different than someone being predestinated to be saved or lost.

However, He did say that once that person accepts Christ, making Him one's Lord and Saviour, that person is *"predestinated to be conformed to the image of God's Son."*

Even then, this does not always happen; however, if the person cooperates with the Lord as it regards his faith, he most definitely will be conformed to the image of the Son.

As well, all other Scriptures that have to do with predestination always refer to *what* is predestinated instead of *whom*.

The great theme of the gospel is always *"whosoever will"* (Rev. 22:17; Jn. 3:16). The idea that God has predestinated some people to go to heaven and some people to go to hell, and there is nothing they have to say in the decision, is not taught in the Word of God.

THE POWER OF GOD

"And I will stretch out My hand, and smite Egypt with all My wonders which I will do in the midst thereof: and after that he will let you go" (Ex. 3:20).

The idea of this verse is, God is almighty, and, thereby, He has the power to do whatever it is that He desires to do. So, in effect, Moses was saying that even though the mighty hand of God was stretched out over Egypt to perform signs and wonders, Pharaoh would continue to be obstinate, refusing to let the children of Israel go. Therefore, the Lord would keep increasing the pressure, even with greater and greater acts of demonstration of power, which would ultimately break down the stubborn heart of the Egyptian monarch. In fact, the greatest miracle of all would be that of the Passover lamb, which would bring about the death of all the firstborn in the land of Egypt. This caused the knees of Pharaoh to buckle, so to speak.

RICHES

"And I will give this people favor in the sight of the Egyptians: and it shall come to pass, that, when you go, you shall not go empty:

"But every woman shall borrow of her neighbor, and of her that sojourns in her house, jewels of silver, and jewels of gold, and raiment: and you shall put them upon your sons, and upon your daughters; and you shall spoil the Egyptians" (Ex. 3:21-22).

I'm certain that when this word was given by Moses to the elders of Israel concerning the great riches that would be heaped upon the Israelites when they left Egypt, these elders must have done a double take. They couldn't imagine Pharaoh letting them go, much less, loading them down with jewels, raiment, etc. However, whatever God says that He will do, irrespective as to how preposterous it might seem at the beginning, how unlikely, and how virtually impossible, to be sure, His Word will come to pass, and will do so exactly as He has said. God cannot lie!

In this, we see the Egyptians willingly paying the Israelites for their hard work and, in effect, paying for what they had stolen from them as well.

One might say that God keeps books on everything. Nothing escapes His notice or attention. To be sure, the bottom line will always come out as it ought to whenever God is overseeing the situation.

"My sins laid open to the rod
"The back which from the law was free;
"And the eternal Son of God
"Received the stripes once due to me."

"No beam was in His eye, nor mote,
"Nor laid to Him was angry blame;
"And yet His cheeks for me were smote
"The cheeks that never blushed for shame."

"I pierced those sacred hands and feet
"That never touched or walked in sin;
"I broke the heart that only beat
"The souls of sinful men to win."

"That sponge of vinegar and gall
"Was placed by me upon His tongue;
"And when derision mocked His call,
"I stood that mocking crowd among."

"And yet His blood was shed for me,
"To be of sin the double cure;
"And balm there flows from Calvary's tree
"That heals my guilt and makes me pure."

CHAPTER FOUR

Moses And The Call Of God

MOSES AND THE CALL OF GOD

"And Moses answered and said, But, behold, they will not believe me, nor hearken unto my voice: for they will say, The LORD has not appeared unto you" (Ex. 4:1).

The hesitating and timid Moses of Mount Horeb was the same courageous and self-reliant Moses who smote the Egyptian dead! His strength then unfitted him as a divine instrument, and now his weakness unfitted him.

God can use neither one nor the other, if the strength is trusted, or if the weakness is sheltered behind as an excuse.

Weakness, as in the case of Moses, budded into unbelief and blossomed into rebellion, but how tenderly God dealt with him!

UNBELIEF

How hard it is to overcome the unbelief of the human heart. How slow we are to believe the promises of God, and how slow we are to have faith in Him. Concerning this,

Mackintosh says: *"The most slender reed that the human eye can see is counted more substantial, by far, as a basis for nature's confidence, than the unseen 'Rock of Ages.'"*

Men will rush to any broken cistern, and do so rapidly, rather than abide by the unseen *"Fountain of Living Waters."*

We watch the church presently as it opts for the broken reed of humanistic psychology, rather than trust the Cross of Christ. That's what it is: a lack of faith in that which Christ has done, so we spring for the pitiful prattle of unredeemed man.

THE CROSS

I believe I can say without fear of contradiction, at least as it regards the modern church, that all erroneous directions lead away from the Cross. That which is biblical, therefore, true and right, always, and without exception, leads to the Cross. So, it's a matter of the Cross, and more particularly, it's a matter of faith.

I maintain that without a proper understanding of the Cross, which, in reality, is a proper understanding of the Word, one cannot really have faith, at least the proper faith that God will honor. Whatever failure we behold in our own personal lives or in the lives of others, and whatever wrong directions are taken, we will find, that is, if we dig enough, that the problem is a lack of faith in Christ and Him crucified (I Cor. 2:2).

Moses raised questions, and still, God answered them, and as we have remarked, each successive question brought out fresh grace.

THE ROD

"And the LORD *said unto him, What is that in your hand? And he said, A rod.*

"And He said, Cast it on the ground. And he cast it on the ground, and it became a serpent; and Moses fled from before it.

"And the LORD *said unto Moses, Put forth your hand, and take it by the tail. And he put forth his hand, and caught it, and it became a rod in his hand:*

"That they may believe that the LORD *God of their fathers, the God of Abraham, the God of Isaac, and the God of Jacob, has appeared unto you"* (Ex. 4:2-5).

Concerning this, Williams says: *"To assure Moses, God gave him two promises and three signs.*

The promises were:

- *'I will be with you.'*
- *'You shall serve God upon this mountain' (Horeb).*

"The three signs were:

- *'The serpent.'*
- *'Leprosy.'*
- *'Blood.'*

"The serpent, Satan and his power; leprosy, sin introduced by him; blood poured out, the wrath of God.

"These three signs taught Moses that the Divine Power, which was to fit him for his mission, could make Satan as

helpless as the rod in his hand, and use him in the accomplishment of God's counsels. Further, that Divine Power could cleanse away sin — a malady as loathsome and incurable as leprosy; and, lastly, that that same Almighty Power would judge with death those who despised that grace."

THE SERPENT

By the rod turning to a serpent, a venomous one at that, Moses, in essence, was being told that he was going to come up against the powers of darkness in Egypt. Egypt was actually ruled by demon spirits, which worked through Pharaoh, the magicians, etc. It was a nation wholly taken over by demon spirits and ruled thereby.

In fact, most of the nations of the world presently fall into the same state. Every religion in the world was and is instituted by demon spirits. Christianity is not a religion, but rather a relationship with Christ; however, much, if not most, of Christianity has degenerated into religion. So, the Lord was showing Moses that which he was coming up against.

The Lord then told Moses to take the snake by the tail, and when he obeyed, it instantly became a rod, the same rod that would be used by God to bring about miracles. This told Moses that he had power over Satan.

He was to catch this serpent by the tail simply because the time for its head to be bruised, as was predicted in the garden of Eden, had not yet come about. That would take place at the Cross (Gen. 3:15).

Therefore, we find here that Moses was going into Egypt with great power, the power of God, behind him, which was greater than all the demon forces of Egypt, even as Egypt was to belatedly see.

Moses was to perform these three signs in the sight of the elders of Israel, and possibly many of the people, as well, which he did.

By the use of the appellative, *"the God of Abraham, the God of Isaac, and the God of Jacob,"* Moses was letting the people know that he was functioning within the boundaries of the same promises that God had given to the patriarchs. God, who is Jehovah, who had appeared unto these three, appeared, as well, to Moses.

LEPROSY

"And the LORD *said furthermore unto him, Put now your hand into your bosom. And he put his hand into his bosom: and when he took it out, behold, his hand was leprous as snow.*

"And he said, Put your hand into your bosom again. And he put his hand into his bosom again; and plucked it out of his bosom, and, behold, it was turned again as his other flesh" (Ex. 4:6-7).

Leprosy is a type of sin, which is the cause of all the problems in the world. The idea is, the Lord was delivering the children of Israel from Egyptian bondage and, as well, would give them a land flowing with milk and honey. It was all for the purpose of bringing the Redeemer into the world, who would address this terrible problem of sin, which He would do at the Cross.

Putting his hand into his bosom and bringing it out and seeing it leprous portrayed to him the terrible horror of the plague of sin that gripped the human race in totality.

THE LEPROUS HAND

Moses was instructed once again to put the leprous hand in his bosom and then take it out. He would find that it had now been made perfectly whole without any sign of leprosy. Thus we see here in this particular *sign* that which Jesus Christ can perform as it regards the salvation of the soul. He can cleanse from all sin, and He alone can cleanse from all sin. There is no other solution to this terrible problem. It is Christ and Christ alone, and more particularly, it is *"Christ and Him crucified"* (I Cor. 1:23).

Who Jesus is and what Jesus did at the Cross is the answer to man's dilemma and, in fact, the only answer to man's dilemma. Man is a moral leper, and anything and everything he might try to do outside of Christ to alleviate the situation leaves him a moral leper. Changing the clothes on a leper in no way changes the leprosy, but that's what man seeks to do.

By having Moses put his hand in his bosom, the Lord was showing Moses that sin is more than an external problem, but rather a problem that begins in the very heart of man, i.e., the bosom. Consequently, external remedies will not suffice. To be sure, man has no remedy, at least within himself, that can go to the heart of the matter. That could only be accomplished by Christ, and it could only be accomplished at the Cross (Gal. 3:13–14).

By leprosy being used as a symbol for sin, we surely should realize how awful, how terrible, and how deadly this problem is. As we have stated and will continue to state, there is only one answer for sin, and that is *"Jesus Christ and Him crucified."*

THE BLOOD

"And it shall come to pass, if they will not believe you, neither hearken to the voice of the first sign, that they will believe the voice of the latter sign.

"And it shall come to pass, if they will not believe also these two signs, neither hearken unto your voice, that you shall take of the water of the river, and pour it upon the dry land: and the water which you take out of the river shall become blood upon the dry land" (Ex. 4:8-9).

The sin caused by Satan is so hideous that it can only be symbolized by the dread disease of leprosy. The idea of this last sign is, the only answer to the serpent, i.e., Satan, and the sin that he causes is the blood, the precious blood of the Lord Jesus Christ. As the serpent was a symbol of Satan and leprosy a symbol of sin, the blood here is a symbol of what Christ would do in order to deliver humanity, and I speak of the shedding of His precious blood on the Cross of Calvary.

THE CROSS OF CALVARY

I'm afraid the church doesn't understand the hideousness and the power of sin, that is, if it believes in sin at all. In fact, if the modern church understood what it is facing, and I continue to speak of Satan and sin, then, to be sure, the modern church would preach the Cross, for there is no other solution.

Ineffably holy in Himself, Jesus had no sin (Heb. 4:15), did no sin (I Pet. 2:22), and knew no sin (II Cor. 5:21). However, in infinite grace, He took our place—all praise to His peerless name — and was made sin for us (II Cor. 5:21). He *"bare our sins in His own body on the tree"* (I Pet. 2:24). Because of this, He was, at that time, in the sight of God what the leper was — defiled, unclean; not inherently so, but by imputation.

In other words, God imputed the defilement to Him exactly as He imputes (gives) righteousness to us.

The leper's place was outside the camp (Lev. 13:46), away from where God dwelt between the mercy seat and the cherubim in the tabernacle. On the Cross Christ was separated for three terrible hours from the thrice-holy God. However, after the awful penalty of sin had been endured, and the work of atonement was finished, the forsaken One is seen again in communion with God — *"Father into Your Hands I commit My Spirit"* evidences that. It was as the *"Holy One"* (Ps. 16:10) He was laid in the sepulchre, not a defiled sinner as some teach.

DESTROYING THE WORKS OF THE DEVIL

Thus, after Moses thrust his leprous hand into his bosom, he drew it forth again perfectly whole — every trace of defilement gone. In their foreshadowings of Christ, then, the first sign intimated that the great Deliverer would *"destroy the works of the Devil"* (I Jn. 3:8). This He would do by His death on the Cross, while the second sign of the leper signified that He would *"take away our sins"* (I Jn. 3:5), which he also accomplished on the Cross.

While the third sign, *"the blood,"* also represented the Cross, we must understand that it is in the form of judgment as much as it is the form of salvation.

If it is to be noticed, the third sign was to be wrought only if the testimony of the first two was refused. It, therefore, tells of the consequences of refusing to believe what the other signs so plainly bore witness to. If man rejects the testimony of God's Word that he is under the dominion of Satan and is depraved by nature and, thereby, refuses the One who alone can deliver from the one and cleanse from the other, nothing but divine judgment awaits him. Deliverance and cleansing can only be done by the shed blood, which speaks of life. Accepted, the blood speaks of life; rejected, the blood speaks of death!

EXCUSES

"And Moses said unto the LORD, O my Lord, I am not eloquent, neither heretofore, nor since You have spoken

unto Your servant: but I am slow of speech, and of a slow tongue" (Ex. 4:10).

God has never called anyone yet who had it all together. In fact, no such human exists.

We can prepare ourselves to a certain extent and should do all that we can, but the final analysis must find the Lord preparing the man as He alone can do.

Furthermore, even as we see here, the Lord doesn't enjoy at all our bringing up our deficiencies, except in the sense of knowing that we have them, and we must depend totally and completely on the Lord to see us through. Otherwise, it is unbelief, which God cannot tolerate.

According to Jewish tradition, Moses had difficulty pronouncing some of the letters, which, in effect, would make him seem to be somewhat stupid. So, if, in fact, this was true, it was an embarrassment to the great lawgiver-to-be.

What was the answer of the Lord concerning the unbelief of Moses? That we will see momentarily.

Any complaint of this nature always registers unbelief, so we should take that into consideration the next time we try to make excuses regarding that which the Lord has told us to do.

THE POWER OF GOD

"And the LORD said unto him, Who has made man's mouth? or who makes the dumb, or deaf, or the seeing, or the blind? have not I the LORD?

"Now therefore go, and I will be with your mouth, and teach you what you shall say" (Ex. 4:11-12).

In answering the complaint of Moses in this fashion, the Lord, in essence, was telling him that whatever his problem might be, it could be easily handled by the power of God. Regarding this, Pulpit says: *"God could and would have cured the defect in Moses' speech, whatever it was; could and would have added eloquence to his other gifts, if he had even at this point yielded himself unreservedly to His guidance and heartily accepted his mission. Nothing is too hard for the Lord."*

The Lord, in essence, was telling Moses that He would teach him what to say and would supply the thought and the language by which to express it. However, the reply in Verse 13 stopped the hand of the Lord.

UNBELIEF

"And he said, O my Lord, send, I pray You, by the hand of him whom You will send" (Ex. 4:13).

The answer given by Moses may be concluded by some to be that of humility; however, it cannot be called humility when we refuse to take the place which God assigns, or to tread the path which His hand marks out for us. That it was not true humility in Moses is obvious from the fact that *"the anger of the LORD was kindled against him."* Actually, it was unbelief!

Concerning this, Mackintosh says: *"Nothing is more dishonoring to God, or more dangerous for us, than a mock humility. When we refuse to occupy a position which the grace of God assigns us, because of our not possessing certain virtues and qualifications, this is not humility, inasmuch as if we could but satisfy our own consciences in reference to such virtues and qualifications, we should then deem ourselves entitled to assume the position."*

The question may be asked, *"How much eloquence would Moses have needed to furnish him for his mission?"* The answer is, *"Without God, no amount of human eloquence would have availed in any case, but with God, the most pitiful stammerer would have proved an efficient minister."*

Unbelief is not humility but thorough pride. It refuses to believe God because it does not find in *self* a reason for believing. This is the very height of presumption. When God speaks, if I refuse to believe on the grounds of something in myself, I make Him a liar (I Jn. 5:10). For instance, when God declares His love, and I refuse to believe because I do not deem myself a sufficiently worthy object, I make Him a liar and exhibit the inherent pride of my heart.

Christ took the sinner's place on the Cross that the sinner might take His place in the glory. Christ got what the sinner deserved that the sinner might get what and who Christ is. Thus, self is totally set aside, and this is true humility.

THE CROSS

No one can be truly humble until he has reached heaven's side of the Cross, and there he finds divine life, divine righteousness, and divine favor. He is done with himself forever, as it regards any expectation of goodness or righteousness, and he feeds upon the princely wealth of another, namely Christ.

As we look at this situation regarding Moses, we must not for a moment think that we would have done any better. The truth is, we probably would not have done nearly as well. So, the way we should look at it is that we learn from the situation here tendered toward us by the Holy Spirit. As a result, we should learn to judge ourselves and to place more implicit confidence in God, to set self aside that He might act in us, through us, and for us. This is the true secret of spiritual power.

THE ANGER OF THE LORD

"And the anger of the LORD *was kindled against Moses, and He said, Is not Aaron the Levite your brother? I know that he can speak well. And also, behold, he comes forth to meet you: and when he sees you, he will be glad in his heart"* (Ex. 4:14).

We are reading here God's reaction to unbelief. Consequently, we must not allow this lesson to be lost on us.

Concerning this, Williams says: *"Despite the promises and signs, the unbelief of Moses' heart ripened into rebellion, and he refused to go; but he immediately consented on being promised the companionship of his brother Aaron. Such is man's heart! Promised the companionship of God, Moses refuses to go, but willingly volunteers if accompanied by a feeble fellow-creature. He would feel safer leaning on the arm of Aaron than leaning on the arm of Jehovah! And yet Aaron was no real help to him, but the contrary; for he made the golden calf. But how full of tender pity was God! He provided this companion, and bade Moses take 'this rod' in his hand wherewith he was to do 'the signs.'"*

AGAIN IT IS UNBELIEF

I think one can say without any fear of contradiction that all sin, in some way, can be traced back to the foundational sin of unbelief. Whatever direction it takes, whatever is done, and whatever the problem, in one way or the other, if inspected closely, one will find unbelief as the real problem.

Also, unbelief can be traced, in one way or the other, to an improper understanding of the Cross. The Scripture plainly says that *"faith comes by hearing, and hearing by the Word of God"* (Rom. 10:17). However, the Word of God is the story of the Cross, while the Cross is the meaning of the Word of God. To properly understand the Word, we must first of all understand the Cross. The believing sinner is saved as he expresses faith in Christ and what Christ has done for us at the Cross, even though he may understand precious little, if anything, about Christ. However, once he is saved, with his faith firmly anchored in Christ, the Holy Spirit then begins to give understanding as it regards the Word. His faith being firmly anchored in Christ will always include what Christ has done at the Cross, that is, if he properly believes. The fact is, the Cross, in a most simplistic way, comes first.

However, at the same time, there is actually no difference in the Cross and the Word. To believe the one, that is, to believe properly, is to believe the other.

AARON

"And you shall speak unto him, and put words in his mouth: and I will be with your mouth, and with his mouth, and will teach you what you shall do.

"And he shall be your spokesman unto the people: and he shall be, even he shall be to you instead of a mouth, and you shall be to him instead of God.

"And you shall take this rod in your hand, wherewith you shall do signs" (Ex. 4:15-17).

It is believed that Aaron was going to see Moses in order to bring him the message that the Pharaoh who had tried to kill him those years before was now dead. However, Verse 27 proclaims the fact that he did not start on the journey till God gave him a special direction.

The Lord would give Moses the words to say, and it would be the duty of Aaron to accept what Moses said as divine.

Possibly to chide Moses, the Lord called attention to the wooden rod in the hand of Moses. He then said to him, *"wherewith you shall do signs."*

In effect, He was telling Moses that He could use anything, even a wooden stick. This shows up greatly the foolishness of Moses in questioning God.

JETHRO

"And Moses went and returned to Jethro his father in law, and said unto him, Let me go, I pray you, and return unto my brethren which are in Egypt, and see whether they be yet alive. And Jethro said to Moses, Go in peace" (Ex. 4:18).

The hardening of Pharaoh's heart doesn't mean that God tampered with Pharaoh's will, but rather by foreknowledge, looked at the heart of the monarch, and knew what Pharaoh would do. God would simply supply the opportunity.

The sun hardens clay and softens wax; so it is with truth. The result is not in the sun (or in God) but in the materials.

In Verse 23, God calls the nation of Israel His son and firstborn as contrasted with the firstborn of Egypt. Pharaoh would understand this terminology fully, for he, himself, was called *"son of Ra"* or *"Beloved of his god."*

At the very beginning, Moses was to tell Pharaoh that if he didn't let the children of Israel go, God would kill his firstborn. So, the monarch was not without warning.

At any point he could have repented, and his firstborn would have been spared, as well as the destruction of Egypt.

Verses 24 through 26 portray the fact of the justness of a just God. Moses would learn that God would judge him before He judged Pharaoh, and that rebellion in the one was the same as rebellion in the other.

THE COMMON AMENITIES OF LIFE

Moses courteously asked leave of Jethro to return to Egypt, for, in a sense, he was Jethro's servant.

Concerning this, Williams says: *"The Midian in which Jethro lived was not the Midian of the Dead Sea region, but of the eastern shore of the Gulf of Akaba. The town of Madyan stands there today; and the Moslems of the town welcome pilgrims on the way to Mecca shouting, 'Come into the city of the brother-in-law of Moses.'"*

Had Moses left for Egypt without first notifying his father-in-law, it would have been grossly discourteous and even the height of ingratitude. This act of Moses manifested his thoughtfulness of others and his appreciation of favors received.

Let writer and reader take this to heart. Spiritual activities, as important as they may be — and nothing could have been more important than this which God had called Moses to do — never absolve us from the common amenities and responsibilities of life. To be a good Christian is to practice Christlikeness, and Christ ever thought of others.

EGYPT

"And the LORD *said unto Moses in Midian, Go, return into Egypt: for all the men are dead which sought your life"* (Ex. 4:19).

From the way the Lord commands Moses here, it would seem that he was still reluctant to go. The Lord would reassure him by telling him that all the men who sought to kill him from 40 years back were now dead. So, there need be no fear from this source.

As we've already stated, we should not read of the reluctance of Moses and think of him as less than ourselves. We must remember that what God was telling him to do was of such magnitude as to defy all description. One can well understand the fear and the trepidation, even though it was wrong.

THE ROD OF GOD

"And Moses took his wife and his sons, and set them upon an animal, and he returned to the land of Egypt: and Moses took the rod of God in his hand" (Ex. 4:20).

His sons were Gershom (Ex. 2:22) and Eliezer, and the latter was probably an infant (Ex. 18:4).

This rod is the same one of Verse 2, which had now become *"the rod of God"* because of the miracle of Verses 3 and 4. The Lord commanded him to take this rod to Egypt.

Think about it, God was going to deliver His people, nearly 3 million strong, from the most powerful nation on earth with one man and a stick.

I think it would be good for us to carefully observe this scene. We have here a man and his older son, most likely walking, while his wife and infant son were riding on the back of a donkey. The man had a rod in his hand, which, of course, was a wooden stick. What other goods they had with them, we aren't told, but they seem to have been traveling very lightly.

The irony of all of this is, this which we see and observe is the instrumentation that God would use, namely Moses, to deliver between 2 and 3 million people from Egyptian bondage. The monarch of that country in no way desired to let them go. To the natural man, this, at the most, would be laughable, and at the least, would be ludicrous. But yet, that's exactly what would happen. Despite the opposition of the mightiest monarch on the face of the earth, nearly 3 million people would come out of Egypt. Furthermore, Egypt would be little more than a wreck when those people departed, and this was the most powerful nation on the face of the earth.

If it is God's will that something be, and God can get a man to believe Him, there is nothing that cannot be done. As the song says, *"What a mighty God we serve!"*

THE HARDENED HEART

"And the LORD said unto Moses, When you go to return into Egypt, see that you do all those wonders before Pharaoh, which I have put in your hand: but I will harden his heart, that he shall not let the people go" (Ex. 4:21).

This particular passage, plus several others similar regarding Pharaoh, has been a source of contention, I suppose, from the very beginning. However, it should not be a problem.

The meaning is, God provided the means which occasioned Pharaoh hardening his own heart.

Among the natural punishments that God has attached to sin would seem to be the hardening of the entire nature of the man who sins. If men do not like to retain God in their knowledge, God gives them up to a reprobate mind (Rom. 1:28). If they resist the Spirit, He takes His Holy Spirit from them (Ps. 51:11). If they sin against light, He withdraws the light. If they stifle their natural affections of kindness, compassion, and the like, it is a law of His providence that those affections shall wither and decay.

Pulpit says: *"This seems to be the 'hardening of the heart' here intended — not an abnormal and miraculous interference with the soul of Pharaoh, but the natural effect upon his soul under God's moral governments of those acts which he willfully and wrongfully committed."*

THE FIRSTBORN

"And you shall say unto Pharaoh, Thus says the LORD, Israel is My son, even My firstborn:

"And I say unto you, Let My son go, that he may serve Me: and if you refuse to let him go, behold, I will slay your son, even your firstborn" (Ex. 4:22-23).

What did the Lord mean by referring to Israel as His firstborn? Israel was the only people and nation that He had adopted because He had taken them into covenant. As a result, they were to be unto Him *"a peculiar people ... above all the nations that are upon the earth"* (Deut. 14:2). Israel's sonship is mentioned here for the first time.

In fact, the whole of the plan of God for the human race was ensconced in these people called *Israelites*. They were raised up for three purposes:

1. To give the world the Word of God, which they did. Every correct standard of righteous law or righteousness in any capacity is based squarely on the Bible.
2. To serve as the womb of the Messiah, which means they would bring the Redeemer into the world, which was predicted even from the fall in the garden of Eden (Gen. 3:15). This they did, as well, even though they did not recognize Him when He came.
3. They were, as well, to evangelize the world, and after a fashion, they succeeded. The Apostle Paul, one might say, began this great effort at world evangelism. In fact, certainly not meaning to take away from the original apostles and others, as well, still, every single person who's ever been saved, and who is redeemed at present, owes a debt of gratitude to the little Jew from Tarsus.

COMING RESTORATION

Chapter 11 of Romans is the most striking chapter in the entirety of the New Testament, even the Bible for that matter, as it regards the fall of Israel and their coming restoration, which will most definitely take place. All the great promises made to the patriarchs and prophets of old will be kept in totality. In other words, Israel is going to ultimately accept

Christ as their Messiah, their Saviour, and their Lord. Zechariah, plus many other prophets, prophesied that this would take place at the second coming (Zech., Chpts. 12–13).

Up front, Moses was to tell Pharaoh that the firstborn of God, namely Israel, must be set free. Refusing that, the next statement, to be sure, is drastic. Without mincing words, the Lord said, *"I will kill your son, even your firstborn."* This meant that the heir to the throne of Egypt would be killed, which the future proved to be the case.

PHARAOH

Pharaoh was not without warning. At any time along the way, he could have repented, and his firstborn would have been spared, as well as the destruction of Egypt. So, it was the mercy of God in speaking to Pharaoh thusly. The choice of what happened was Pharaoh's and not God's. The Israelites belonged to God; they didn't belong to Pharaoh. They were God's personal property. They were His people, and He had the right to take them out.

The religion of Egypt looked at their firstborn as carrying on their name for each family, guaranteeing its success in this life and even in the afterlife, and more particularly, the afterlife. If the firstborn was cut off before maturity or before the father died, all of this would be interrupted. So, the idea that the God of the Hebrews was to kill every firstborn in the land of Egypt, even that of the cattle, etc., was about the worst thing that Pharaoh could hear. But yet, his stubborn, obstinate, and hardened heart refused to believe the announcement of Moses because he reasoned that the gods of Egypt were greater than the God of the Hebrews. He was to have a rude awakening!

THE LESSON THAT MOSES WAS TO LEARN

"And it came to pass by the way in the inn, that the LORD *met him, and sought to kill him.*

"Then Zipporah took a sharp stone, and cut off the foreskin of her son, and cast it at his feet, and said, Surely a bloody husband are you to me.

"So He let him go: then she said, A bloody husband you are, because of the circumcision" (Ex. 4:24-26).

The rite of circumcision was the seal of the covenant that God had given to Abraham some 400 years before (Gen. 17:10–14).

The rite of circumcision included the separation of flesh and the shedding of blood, both of which typified Christ and the Cross, in other words, what He would do in order to redeem fallen humanity. Consequently, it was very important that this particular commandment be obeyed to the letter because of its symbolism.

It seems that the son of which they were speaking here was not Gershom, who was the oldest, and who had, no doubt, been circumcised, but rather Eliezer, who was an infant, and probably several months old.

Evidently Zipporah was opposed to the rite of circumcision, seemingly thinking that it was a barbarous act. So, we find here that the wife of Moses was not too very much in sympathy with the things of God. So, Moses, not desiring to create a family problem, had evidently acquiesced to his wife and had neglected to circumcise the baby boy.

Abruptly, the Scripture says that the Lord suddenly appeared to Moses and because of his neglect in circumcising the little boy, the Lord threatened to kill the child. It is a strong statement and must not be dismissed hastily.

CIRCUMCISION

Why was the matter this serious?

Concerning this, Williams says: *"Moses was commanded to announce to Pharaoh that Jehovah, the God of Israel, was about to slay his son. But Moses had to learn that disobedience and rebellion in him was just as hateful as in Pharaoh; and that God, because of His nature, must judge with death, sin wherever found.*

"On approaching Egypt, therefore, this Holy God sought to judge his little boy, Eliezer, because of Moses' disobedience in not having had him circumcised, as God had commanded. The passage throws a great light upon the inner life of Moses. It may be assumed, from what is related, that he yielded to the wishes of his wife in this matter, though he knew he was disobeying God. The particulars are not fully given because the Holy Spirit did not think this necessary, but evidently in order to save the child's life, and urged to it by Moses, she circumcised him herself, and then with anger

and passion declared that her husband's religion was a reli-gion of blood, i.e., 'of blood-stained rites.'

"Thus Moses had to learn that God would judge him before He judged Pharaoh, and that rebellion in the one was the same as rebellion in the other; and this lesson must have enabled Moses to proclaim this dreadful truth with the force of a personal experience."

THE CROSS

Williams continues to say, and I continue to quote: *"This is a moral principle which Romans 6, Colossians 2, and many other Scriptures teach. Christians, under the new covenant, are circumcised in the death of Jesus Christ; that is, we 'die' as to our old nature. We then go forth with a message of death and of life; but we must have a personal experience of the bitterness, to the natural will, of that spiritual circumcision. We must consent to 'die' if we would be effective messengers of the Cross."*

This is all very dear to me personally.

Until I understood the part the Cross plays in our sanctification experience, in other words, our daily living before the Lord, I could not live a victorious life, and neither can anyone else. The sadness is, very few in the modern church understand that which I've just mentioned, so that means that almost all of the modern church is living far less than God intends. This means that they do not have nearly all the first-fruits they can have according to what Jesus did at the Cross.

God has one prescribed order of victory, not five, not three, not two, just one. If we follow that prescribed order, we will reap the result, which is victory on a perpetual basis. If we ignore what the Lord has said, even as Moses did regarding the circumcision of his little son, or if we function in unbelief as it regards the Cross, because the Cross is the prescribed order, the results will be disastrous. It can be no other way.

This which the Lord has shown me, even though it incorporates the entirety of the new covenant, I believe can be reduced down to the following three points. Of course, such an abbreviation leaves much to be desired; still, it will give the reader a working knowledge of God's prescribed way.

GOD'S PRESCRIBED ORDER OF VICTORY

Before I give that prescribed order, I want the reader to understand that the Cross of Christ is not a mere doctrine. In fact, it is the foundation of all doctrine. Every doctrine in the Bible is built squarely on the Cross of Christ. If any doctrine is proposed by men, and it doesn't have the Cross as its foundation, that doctrine, pure and simple, is wrong.

I think that Jesus looked at what He did on the Cross, the great price that He paid, in fact, that which was planned from before the foundation of the world, as far more than mere doctrine. No, as stated, while it may be spoken of as a doctrine, the Cross of Christ is, in fact, the foundation of all doctrine. That must be understood up front.

It is that simply because it was the very first doctrine, one might say, formulated in the mind of the Godhead, which was done even before the foundation of the world (I Pet. 1:18-20).

1. THE CROSS OF CHRIST

The first thing the believer must understand is, everything that we receive from God, and I mean everything, comes to us exclusively by and through the Cross of Christ. In other words, the Cross is what made everything possible. I speak of salvation, the baptism with the Holy Spirit, victorious Christian living, deliverance, divine healing, financial prosperity, and emotional well-being, in fact, victory in every capacity.

Let us look at the Cross in this fashion: If all of this had stopped at the deity of Christ, and to be sure, Christ is God, the great salvation plan would be incomplete. As God, Jesus had no beginning, has always been, and will always be, and is unformed, unmade, and uncreated. Even though His deity was an absolute necessity, had it stopped there, not a single sinner would have ever been saved.

As well, His virgin birth was an absolute necessity; nevertheless, had it stopped there, not one single person would have ever been saved.

His perfect life falls into the same category, but that alone would have saved no one.

His miracles were a necessity, but even though they were grand and glorious, they could save no one.

To be sure, the Lord, being almighty, could have effected salvation with just the wave of His hand. He is almighty and all-knowing, but to be true to His nature and character, which He always will be, He had to go to the Cross.

For salvation to be what it should be, it remained for Jesus to go to the Cross, which, in reality, was the reason that He came (Jn. 1:29). He went to the Cross in order that the terrible sin debt might be paid, which was paid with the shedding of His precious blood, actually, the giving of Himself in sacrifice.

So, it is the Cross that has made and does make everything possible as it regards God's relationship with man (Gen. 3:15; 15:6; Rom. 6:3–5, 11, 14; Eph. 2:13–18; Col. 2:14–15).

2. YOUR FAITH

It is not the quantity of faith that is so important, but rather the object in which our faith is placed, which must be the Cross, and that being the case, that is quality faith. Inasmuch as the Cross is the instrument used whereby all things are given to us by God, that is where we must place our faith and not allow it to be moved to other things. That's the reason we keep saying, even to the degree of being overly repetitious, that we must make certain that the object of our faith is always the Cross. Satan will fight harder here than he does anywhere else in order to move our faith from the finished work of Christ to other things. To be sure, he really doesn't care too very much what those other things might be, or even how holy they might be in their own right. As long as the believer doesn't have his faith in the Cross of Christ, Satan knows that such a believer will live a life of spiritual defeat and, more than likely, defeat in every other manner as well.

If we ask most Christians to explain faith, most really would not understand how to do that. They would answer with the statement, *"I have faith in God," "I have faith in His Word,"* etc. They might even say, *"Jesus died for me, and I believe that."* All of these things are right as far as they go; however, they really don't say very much.

The believer must understand that to properly comprehend faith, he must ever have the Cross as its object. Always and without exception, when Paul spoke of faith, he was speaking of having faith in Christ and what Christ did at the Cross. In fact, the word *faith* carries such a power that the Christian experience is oftentimes referred to as *"the faith"* (Gal. 2:20; 5:6).

The truth is, everyone in the world has faith. While it's not faith in God and His Word, still, it is faith, but it's not faith that God will recognize. In fact, He doesn't even recognize most of the faith held by those who are a part of the church, or who claim salvation. Their faith is in things other than the Cross; consequently, such faith is that which God cannot recognize or condone. Unfortunately, the faith that's been taught and practiced in the last few decades, at least for the most part, has been faith in things other than the Cross. As a result, it is useless faith or worthless faith. Let us say it again: it is only faith in Christ and the Cross that is true biblical faith, therefore, the faith that God will recognize (I Cor. 1:17–18, 23; 2:2, 5).

When a believer says that he has faith in the Word, that is a true statement. However, what the believer must understand is, the entirety of the story of the Bible is the story of Jesus Christ and Him crucified. In one way or the other, everything in the Word of God, every happening, every circumstance, and every situation, all and without question point in some way to Christ and the Cross. In fact, every single sacrifice offered of a young lamb before the Cross typified Christ and what He would do at the Cross.

3. THE HOLY SPIRIT

Anything and everything that we receive from the Lord not only comes through the Cross but is always superintended by the Holy Spirit. One might say that Jesus Christ is the source of all things we receive from God, while the Cross is the means, but the Holy Spirit is the One who gives it to us.

The Holy Spirit alone can develop fruit within our lives, *"the fruit of the Spirit"* (Gal. 5:22–23). Of course, that, as well, is made possible by the Cross. The truth is, if it's from God, it is the Holy Spirit who makes it real to us, thereby, guaranteeing the fruit of that which Jesus paid for at the Cross. Actually, Jesus lives in us by and through the Holy Spirit, who lives constantly within our hearts and lives (I Cor. 3:16; Gal. 2:20; Jn. 16:13–15).

Concerning this, Paul said, *"For the preaching of the Cross is to them that perish foolishness; but unto us which are saved it is the power of God"* (I Cor. 1:18).

The power of God is always ensconced in the Holy Spirit (Acts 1:8). Now, many believers think if they are baptized with the Holy Spirit with the evidence of speaking with other tongues, which definitely is scriptural (Acts 2:4), this means that the Holy Spirit will do all types of things for them.

While that is definitely a giant step forward and, as well, an absolute necessity for every believer, still, have you noticed that Spirit-filled people suffer failure just about as much as the non-Spirit-baptized variety? So, what's wrong?

POTENTIAL

When the Holy Spirit comes into our hearts and lives in a baptism of power, which He definitely does when we are baptized with the Spirit, He, in fact, can do many things. However, all of these things are potential and not necessarily factual. To be sure, He is no respecter of persons and will do for one what He has done for the other, but just because one is baptized with the Spirit, it does not mean that one is home free, so to speak. The potential is there, but at that stage, the potential only.

The Holy Spirit doesn't demand much of us, but He does demand that we exhibit faith in the Cross of Christ and keep our faith in that finished work.

He said: *"There is therefore now no condemnation to them which are in Christ Jesus, who walk not after the flesh, but after the Spirit."*

He then said: *"For the law of the Spirit of life in Christ Jesus has made me free from the law of sin and death"* (Rom. 8:1–2).

Romans 8:2 tells us that the Holy Spirit works exclusively within the parameters of the finished work of Christ. That's what is meant by the term, *in Christ Jesus.* As well, the Holy Spirit will not work outside of those parameters, i.e., will not work outside of the Cross.

SPIRITUAL ADULTERY

In the first four verses of Chapter 7 of Romans, and I'll be brief, Paul, in effect, tells us that believers who are married to Christ must receive everything we need from Him and Him alone! This is done by having faith exclusively in Christ and what Christ has done for us at the Cross. If we veer outside of those parameters and begin to have faith in law, which speaks of *"works,"* we are then being unfaithful to our Lord, and God then looks at us as a spiritual adulterer (Rom. 7:3).

I should think that it would be understood by all that it's a very serious thing for God to conclude us as a spiritual adulterer. This simply means that we are being unfaithful to our Lord. He has all that we need, which He furnishes to us through the Cross. However, if we attempt to live this life by placing our faith in other things, then we place ourselves in a very precarious position indeed.

Now, let me ask this question: If the Lord considers such a person a spiritual adulterer, which He definitely does, do you honestly think that the Holy Spirit is going to help such a person in his endeavors that are going wrong? I don't think so!

To be sure, if we are to live the life we must live, we must have the help of the Holy Spirit in every capacity. He will help us only in the realm of the Cross of Christ and our faith in that finished work.

WALKING AFTER THE SPIRIT

So, that's the reason that many Spirit-filled people fail the Lord. To be sure, the Holy Spirit doesn't leave them, but at the same time, He doesn't help them because He cannot be involved in that which God clearly labels as *adulterous* (Rom. 7:1–4). To have His help, which we must have because He is God and He can do anything, we simply have to express faith in Christ and Christ exclusively, which refers to what he did at the Cross for us. Doing that, the Holy Spirit will bring about total victory within our hearts and lives because that is walking after the Spirit, and then sin will not have dominion over us (Rom. 6:14; 8:1).

It seems that the rite of circumcision was an offense to the wife of Moses just as the Cross is an offense to many today (Gal. 5:11).

So, there you have it, even though it is in abbreviated form. It is the Cross, our faith, and the Holy Spirit.

AARON

"And the LORD said to Aaron, Go into the wilderness to meet Moses. And he went, and met him in the mount of God, and kissed him.

"And Moses told Aaron all the words of the LORD who had sent him, and all the signs which he had commanded him" (Ex. 4:27-28).

Verses 27 and 28 record the Lord telling Aaron, *"Go into the wilderness to meet Moses."* Aaron met Moses at Mount Sinai perhaps very shortly after Moses received the revelation of the burning bush. The brothers had been separated for some 40 years.

Verses 29 through 31 record the first spiritual revival of the children of Israel since they had been in Egyptian bondage, which was a span of time of some 215 years.

The Scripture says, *"They bowed their heads and worshipped."* This is a perfect description of every moving of the Holy Spirit. God will do signs, and then, if the people believe, the Spirit of God will fall and result in the worship of the Lord.

Aaron evidently had come from Egypt and had not seen his brother in 40 years. So, this meeting would be one of great joy. It would be a scene of sweet brotherly love and union.

The two men conversed, with Moses telling his older brother of the great things the Lord had shown him and told him. Now Aaron was to find out that he was to be the spokesman for Moses as it regarded the tremendous confrontation, which would take place quite a number of times, between Moses and the monarch of Egypt.

Aaron, like Moses, was barred from entering Canaan at the end of the wilderness wanderings. He died and was buried on Mount Hor, on the Edomite border, and his functions and vestments as the high priest of Israel passed to his son, Eleazar (Num. 20:22-28). Actually, the priesthood in Israel came to be known comprehensively as *"the sons of Aaron."*

THE ARRIVAL IN EGYPT

"And Moses and Aaron went and gathered together all the elders of the children of Israel" (Ex. 4:29).

The Scripture is silent regarding the trip to Egypt. The Scripture seems to indicate that Moses sent his wife and children back to Jethro (Ex. 18:2). To be frank, considering what he had to do, that was the prudent thing to have done.

The journey from Horeb, for that's where Aaron met Moses, to Goshen probably occupied some weeks. It seems that immediately upon arriving in Goshen, the two brothers, in obedience to the divine command, proceeded at once to gather together all the elders of Israel. This would have included the heads of the tribes, plus other important men, who, no doubt, numbered several hundreds, and possibly even several thousands.

THE SIGNS

"And Aaron spoke all the words which the LORD *had spoken unto Moses, and did the signs in the sight of the people"* (Ex. 4:30).

It seems that Moses performed all the signs concerning the serpent, the leprous hand, and the blood in the sight of the elders, and all was observed by them. They then went and gathered together a tremendously large group of people, with Moses once again doing the signs *"in the sight of the people."*

This was God's time, with the people in an entirely different frame of mind than they had been those years before. Besides that, Moses was an entirely different man now than he had been then.

FAITH

"And the people believed: and when they heard that the LORD *had visited the children of Israel, and that He had looked upon their affliction, then they bowed their heads and worshipped"* (Ex. 4:31).

All of this shows that during the time between the death of Joseph and the arrival of Moses for the purpose of deliverance, the people had at least been taught some things about God. Their situation in the wilderness would prove to be extremely negative, with none of the adults going into the Promised Land, with the exception of Joshua and Caleb.

Still, there seems to have been some semblance of instruction given during the time in question. Their *"worshipping"* even as they did proves this.

When God works, every barrier must give way. Moses had said, *"the people will not believe me,"* but the question was not whether they would believe him, but whether they would believe God. Their faith reached out at this time, and, in fact, they did believe.

"O sacred Head, now wounded,
"With grief and shame weighed down;
"Now scornfully surrounded
"With thorns, Your only crown."

"How pale You are with anguish,
"With sore abuse and scorn;
"How does that visage languish,
"Which once was bright as morn!"

"O Lord of life and glory,
"What bliss till now was Yours!
"I read the wondrous story;
"I joy to call You mine."

"What You, my Lord, have suffered
"Was all for sinners' gain;
"Mine, mine was the transgression,
"But Yours the deadly pain."

"What language shall I borrow
"To thank You, dearest Friend,
"For this Your dying sorrow,
"Your pity without end?"

"O, make me Yours forever;
"And, should I fainting be,
"Lord, let me never, never
"Outlive my love for You."

"Be near me when I'm dying,
"O, show Your Cross to me;
"And to my succor flying,
"Come, Lord, to set me free."

"These eyes, new faith receiving,
"From Jesus shall not move,
"For he who dies believing,
"Dies safely through Your love."

CHAPTER FIVE

The Way Satan Works

THE WAY SATAN WORKS

"And afterward Moses and Aaron went in, and told Pharaoh, Thus saith the LORD *God of Israel, Let My people go, that they may hold a feast unto Me in the wilderness"* (Ex. 5:1).

The close of Chapter 4 presents the people worshipping in believing joy. The close of Chapter 5, which we will ultimately see, sets before the reader the same people filled with unbelieving bitterness. The glad tidings of salvation is one thing; the struggle against the power that tries to keep the soul in bondage is quite another. Now, that is a powerful statement and should be read very carefully. It is so important that I want to quote it again: *"The glad tidings of salvation is one thing; the struggle against the power that tries to keep the soul in bondage is quite another."*

Satan will not easily let his captive go free, and God permits the bitter experience of his power in order to exercise and strengthen faith.

It is good for a man to learn painfully, and painful it is, the nature of sin's dominion and his absolute helplessness in the grip of that monarch.

PHARAOH

According to many authorities, the Pharaoh at that time was Meneptah, the son and successor of Rameses II. History records that he was a weak individual, but because of certain events, had an exalted opinion of himself.

Egypt had been invaded recently, actually at the beginning of his reign, which had been met and completely repulsed. However, it was not by his skill at the head of his army, but rather by the skill of his generals. Nevertheless, Meneptah claimed to be in direct communication with the Egyptian gods, who revealed themselves to him in visions, which he used as an excuse not to lead his army. Still, he counted the successes gained by his generals as his own and conducted himself as the leader. Such was the man before whom Moses and Aaron appeared.

THE FIRST TACTIC OF SATAN

It made no mind, at least to Pharaoh, that God, who had created the heavens and the earth, and who was capable of doing anything, had said, *"Let My people go."* Pharaoh was not about to relent upon that word alone.

You as a believer should understand that the Word of God claims our victory in totality. However, just because the Word claims it, and just because it is most definitely real, the enemy of your soul will not give ground easily.

The truth is this: Sin is the problem, and the Cross is the only answer for sin. The Message of the Cross proclaiming the answer is going out all over the world. To be sure, Satan will ultimately yield, but he will not do it without a fight.

A PERSONAL EXPERIENCE

Not so long after the Lord began to open up to me the great Message of the Cross, which is an astounding revelation to say the least, Satan began to plague me with one of his lies of darkness. Please understand, what the Lord gave me was not new, in fact, the Cross is the oldest doctrine known to man, that is, if we could refer to it as a doctrine (I Pet. 1:18-20).

The Evil One began to tell me that while there may be a few Christians who are troubled with problems, the far greater majority is doing well. In other words, he was saying that there was no need for the Message of the Cross. He was telling me that the situation was not nearly as bad as I thought it was, and so, in essence, I was preaching to the choir.

I did not say anything to anyone about what was taking place in my spirit, but it was powerful to say the least. I would lay awake at night wondering, *"Is this Message of the Cross really that necessary?"* When you look at the outward, most Christians seem to be looking good and doing well, but is that the real case?

It was a Sunday night, and Donnie was preaching. He was not preaching concerning the deliverance of the children of Israel from Egyptian bondage, but for some purpose and reason in his delivery, he quoted what Moses said to Pharaoh, *"Let My people go."*

When he said that, the Spirit of God came all over me. The Lord spoke graphically to my soul, stating, *"The truth is, My people are in the same condition that the children of Israel were in as it regards being slaves to Pharaoh that time so long ago."* It was a startling revelation. To think that the people of God at this particular time are in the same condition that the children of Israel were in Egypt is shocking indeed! But yet, I knew that it was the Lord speaking this word unto me. He was telling me that the situation was far, far worse than even I realized.

ANOTHER EXPERIENCE

I have always been fearful of claiming that the Lord had said something to me when it really was not the Lord. Consequently, I have always insisted that the Lord make His Word real, very real to me, in order that when I say, *"thus saith the Lord,"* it is really the Lord speaking and not something merely out of my mind.

This of which I speak took place a short time ago. One particular morning while in prayer, just before I went to the studio for our morning program, *The Message of the Cross,* I asked the Lord to give me a sign because of certain events.

I prayed, *"If what I am teaching and preaching is exactly what You want and is exactly according to Your Word, please do something in the program to let me know that."*

I went on to state, *"Lord, I don't want to preach anything, to teach anything, to say anything, claiming it's You when in reality it isn't."*

I went on praying about other things and forgot what I had asked the Lord.

The program began without me thinking of the situation at all. In other words, what I had asked the Lord did not at all come to my mind. The program was coming down to the end, with only about five minutes left. Once again, I had not thought of that which I had requested of the Lord.

Loren Larson, who was with me on the program that day, plus several others, made a statement which I do not now remember. At any rate, I instantly sensed the presence of the Lord, and I mean in a powerful way.

John Rosenstern was sitting to my left and began to sob as the Spirit of God began to move.

I began to minister to the people, urging them to believe the Lord as His presence covered our efforts, and I knew the Lord was doing something for our audience all over the world.

Still, what I had asked the Lord did not come to me. The program ended, and I walked through the building and walked outside, closing the door behind me and going toward the administration building.

All of a sudden, the presence of the Lord came over me again, and the Lord said, *"You asked Me to show you beyond the shadow of a doubt that what you were teaching was right, and I answered your prayer. I gave you My presence, and there is nothing greater than that, nothing that could be a greater sign than that."*

I stood there that day outside of the studio with tears in my eyes, knowing that the Lord had wondrously answered.

Ladies and gentlemen, the only answer for sin, and I mean the only answer, is the Cross of Christ. It's not one of several answers; it is the only answer.

What I am saying is a strong statement, but I know it to be true: The modern church being in worse condition today, or at least as bad as the children of Israel were under Egyptian bondage, is quite a statement. I am speaking of those who truly love the Lord and who truly are born again, with most of them Spirit-filled. As I said, it is a strong statement, but I know it is true. There are millions all over the world that are crying to God for help. They are being overcome by the powers of darkness. They have struggled against Satan with every iota of their strength, all to no avail.

The word that we quoted a short time ago needs to be repeated: *"The glad tidings of salvation is one thing; the struggle against the power that tries to keep the soul in bondage is quite another."*

To be sure, the Lord has stated exactly as He did some 2,500 years ago, *"Let My people go."* However, just because God has said it, and He most definitely has, it doesn't mean that Satan is going to yield and buckle. If you, the believer, will not quit, will not give up, and will keep believing, victory is going to be yours, and it will be a victory such as you have never known before. In this particular chapter, we are going to tell you how that Satan works, and please believe me, he is working the same way that he did those long, long years ago.

THE HOLY SPIRIT

If it is to be noticed, the Holy Spirit, in giving Moses direction regarding the Sacred Text, in no way recognized the splendor of Egypt, even though the trappings of grandeur were, no doubt, copiously obvious, with the throne a dazzling object of magnificence. This was the throne of Pharaoh, the mightiest nation on the face of the earth at that time, therefore, the mightiest monarch.

For a few moments, I want the reader to imagine the scene that must have presented itself to Moses and Aaron as they stood before Pharaoh. Quite possibly, some of the elders of Israel were with them. These two prophets of God stood there in their simple shepherd's garb, standing before a man graced by every bauble of jewelry and the finest of garments, which would feed his ego.

There is a possibility that Moses was very familiar with this palace and even may have been raised in this domain. In fact, the throne on which Pharaoh was now seated could have been his. If so, what a step down it would have been.

When he looked at Pharaoh, the scene that met his eyes must have been graphic. Very probably, on Pharaoh's head would have been the replica of a coiled cobra made of gold. The cobra's head, with two rubies for its eyes, would have protruded like a hood over the head of the monarch. The cobra was one of the gods of Egypt.

They would now confront Pharaoh in person. His temper toward the Hebrews was well-known; his heartless cruelty had been frequently displayed. Pink says: *"It was, therefore, no small trial of their faith and courage to beard the lion in his den."* Pink goes on to say: *"The character of the message they were to deliver to him was not calculated to compromise or pacify. They were to tell him in no uncertain terms that the Lord God required him to let these people go whom he held in slavery, and hold a feast unto Jehovah in the wilderness."*

THUS SAITH THE LORD ...

As well, they went before this monarch knowing that the Lord had told them that He would harden Pharaoh's heart, which meant they would be met with no favorable response.

The Lord had used the term to Moses, *thus saith the* LORD, that he was to speak to Pharaoh when, in fact, he would stand in his presence. As it was now uttered in the presence of the monarch, the words, *"thus saith the* LORD *God,"* were used here for the first time. It would be used untold numbers of times in the coming years and centuries, but this was the first.

In this statement, God identified Himself with this beleaguered band of slaves by saying, *"thus saith the Lord God of Israel."* As a result, the might and power of heaven were now registered on the side of Israel. Irrespective of whom they might be, where they might be, or whom their captors might be, the opposing party could not win. *"Thus saith the Lord,"* presents itself as the death knell to all who would stand in the way of the will of God. In fact, a short time later when Israel would leave Egypt, this mighty nation, possibly the most powerful on the face of the earth at that time, would be left a wreck. If God has spoken, only fools would dare oppose Him or the one or ones whom He sponsors.

A FEAST

Careful attention should be paid to the terms of their demand. The Lord had already promised Moses that he and the children of Israel would worship God on Mount Sinai (Ex. 3:12), and to be sure, that was far more than a three days' journey from Egypt.

So, why did not Moses plainly tell Pharaoh that he must relinquish all claims on the Hebrews, thereby, giving them permission to leave his land for good?

Even though it is not mentioned in the first verse, in Verse 3, the Lord had told Moses to ask for a three days' journey into the desert where they would there sacrifice unto the Lord.

Pink answers this question: *"God is entering upon a controversy with Pharaoh and with Egypt. He is about to judge them; and, in order that they may be judged, they must first be revealed to themselves and to all men. Had they been asked to suffer the Israelites to depart from Egypt, so large a demand might have seemed to others, and certainly would have appeared to the Egyptians themselves, as so unreasonable as to justify their refusal.*

Pink continues: *"A request is made, therefore, against which no charge of the kind can be brought. A three days' journey into the wilderness need not have taken the Israel-ites much beyond the Egyptian frontier. It was also a per-fectly reasonable request, even to heathen nations, that they should be permitted to worship their God after the accepted manner. Consequently, the heart of Pharaoh and of his people was, therefore, revealed in their scornful refusal of a perfectly reasonable request. In this way they committed themselves to what was manifestly unjust; and in proceed-ing against them, God was consequently justified even in their own eyes."*

THE JUDGMENT OF GOD

I think it can be said that God has never judged a people whom He has not first dealt with in this very way, or at least in a similar way. For instance, Thomas Carlyle traces the fear-ful blow which fell upon the clergy and the aristocracy in the French Revolution to the murder of St. Bartholomew. France had sought to crush the Reformation as Egypt had sought to crush Israel.

Spain is another case in point: she dug the grave for her greatness and her fame in the establishment of her Inquisi-tion, which saw untold thousands slaughtered because of their stand for Christ or refusal to recognize the pope.

Frances and I stood in Toledo, Spain, and observed the torture racks that were used to take the lives of untold num-bers of people, who died in a most horrible fashion. As I looked at these instruments of torture, all perpetrated in the name of religion, the words drummed upon my mind and my soul: *"Be not deceived; God is not mocked: for whatsoever a man sows, that shall he also reap"* (Gal. 6:7).

But yet, we have to go even further to find the full reason and explanation for this request as offered by God to Pharaoh.

THE MERCY AND GRACE OF THE LORD

Do we not see in all of this the mercy, the grace, and the love of God? God is all-powerful, meaning that He can do anything. Pharaoh was no more to God than a flea on a dog, so to speak, that is, if we are to compare power. He didn't have to ask Pharaoh anything. Above all, he didn't have to ask him time and time again. He could have done what He desired to do (what He wanted to do), and could have done so instantly, and there would have been absolutely nothing that Pharaoh could have done about it.

However, God never uses His power capriciously. He always seeks the best for men. If they will not yield to His ways and will, He will then take stronger measures, but He always deals with patience, mercy, and grace.

He had every right to do what He did. He was not demanding anything even remotely unreasonable. These Israelites were His people. He had nurtured them and brought them to this present place and position. Besides that, Pharaoh had almost worked them to death as slaves, had used them unmercifully, and had abused them to a great degree, which, in effect, added insult to injury.

Let it ever be known that when we touch those who belong to God, we have, in effect, touched God. This entire scenario of God's dealings with Pharaoh should be a prime example of this of which I speak.

THE PURPOSE OF GOD

All of this battle that we see played out before us was definitely to deliver Israel from their bitter bondage; however, it was definitely not merely for that. Neither was it fought and won solely that Israel might be able to go forth and possess the land promised to her fathers. That was important, but there were reasons which were greater.

The greater reason was that Israel was redeemed to be God's people. Her one mission was and is to serve Jehovah. The conflict was being waged over the destiny of a race, its place in history, and in the service of humanity. Was Israel to be slave or priest, or Egypt's beast of burden or the anointed of Jehovah? That was the great question. Was it possible that God could have done other than put that question, written large and clear, in the forefront of this great controversy?

So, we find God acting here, not in wrath, but in mercy. This is ever His way. Before He would drown the world by water, He would send forth Enoch as a herald of this coming storm long before the flood descended upon the antediluvians. He sent forth Noah as a preacher of righteousness years before the first drop of rain began to fall, at least as it regarded the flood.

GRACE AND LONGSUFFERING

Even regarding Israel centuries later, He sent forth one prophet after another before He banished them into captivity. Later, He sent forth His own Son, followed by the apostles, before He used the Roman Tenth Legion to destroy Jerusalem in A.D. 70.

So it is presently. God is now dealing in grace and longsuffering, sending forth His servants far and wide, bidding men to flee from the wrath to come. However, this day of salvation is rapidly drawing to a close, and once the Lord rises from His place at God's right hand, the door of mercy will be shut, and the storm of God's righteous anger will burst upon this world.

We are not without warning. The book of Revelation, plus even the stentorian tones of the Master Himself in Matthew, Chapter 24, proclaim to us in no uncertain terms that judgment is just ahead. So, the world is without excuse. Preachers can deny the validity of the book of Revelation, but its message throbs a little louder with each passing day, and only a fool will ignore its warnings.

WHO IS THE LORD?

"And Pharaoh said, Who is the Lord, *that I should obey His voice to let Israel go? I know not the* Lord, *neither will I let Israel go"* (Ex. 5:2).

Let it be known that in reference to His elect, nothing can ever satisfy God but their entire emancipation from the yoke of bondage. *"Loose him and let him go"* is really the grand motto in God's gracious dealings with those who, though held in bondage by Satan, are, nevertheless, the objects of His eternal love.

Mackintosh said: *"When we contemplate Israel amid the brick kilns of Egypt, we behold a graphic figure of the condition of every child of Adam's fallen race by nature. There they were, crushed beneath the enemy's galling yoke, and having no power to deliver themselves. The mere mention of the word 'liberty' only caused the oppressor to bind his captives with a stronger fetter, and to lade them with a still more grievous burden. Consequently, it was absolutely necessary that deliverance should come from without."*

Even the smallest thing that we allow in our lives that is not under the control of the Holy Spirit is completely sufficient to account for spiritual confusion. That statement is so compelling that we must say it again: *"Even the smallest thing that we allow in our lives that is not under the control of the Holy Spirit is completely sufficient to account for spiritual confusion."*

The business of the Holy Spirit is to make us free from every binding force as it regards the world, the flesh, and the Devil. That's the reason that the Holy Spirit had Paul to write: *"For the flesh lusteth against the Spirit, and the Spirit against the flesh: and these are contrary the one to the other: so that you cannot do the things that you would"* (Gal. 5:17).

THE SUPREMACY OF THE FLESH

The Holy Spirit cannot tolerate the supremacy of the flesh in anything simply because He knows the terrible destructive force that such possession will bring about. Forever, the Holy Spirit is pitted against the flesh, and there will never be quarter asked or given.

The manner in which Paul used the word *flesh* refers to our own ability, strength, and way. This, of course, speaks of man going his way without the Spirit, and attempting to do by his own strength and ability that which the Spirit alone can do.

It does not lie within man to make himself holy or righteous. It simply cannot be done. The holdovers from the fall guarantee the failure of such an effort. Not even the believer to whom Paul writes can effect by our own personal ability this work within our lives. This is true even though we are a new creation and baptized with the Holy Spirit.

Oh, how many of us have had to learn this the hard way? How many times have we beaten upon this anvil with our hammers of strength and power? But alas, sooner or later, the hammers break, but the anvil remains. To be sure, the anvil will not move by our strength, but it will move and, in fact, must move as the power of the Holy Spirit is registered against it. Irrespective as to how great Pharaoh must be, he is doomed to fail, and God will not tolerate a partial deliverance, only that which is total.

THE PRESENCE OF GOD

As I dictate these notes, I sense greatly the presence of God. I sense the Holy Spirit saying through me that for all who read these words, if we will only follow the great Word of God and put our faith and trust in Christ and what He did at the Cross, victory can be ours, and in totality. As we have stated, God will not condone a partial victory; it must be a total victory, as every victory by the Lord is a total victory.

How many times have the tears blanketed your cheeks? How many times has despair filled your heart? How many times have you failed and then have said, *"I will try again"*?

You can be free. There is no doubt about it! What Jesus did at the Cross addressed every single problem that man might have. He left nothing undone, hence, that which He did is referred to as the *"finished work."* He is the *"last Adam,"* which means there will never again be the need for another one.

Your victory is in the Cross. More particularly, it's in what Jesus did there because He did it for you. God means for you to be completely free. Jesus didn't die on that Cross in order that you might have a partial victory, but He died on that Cross that you might have victory in every capacity and perpetually.

WHO IS THE LORD?

Pharaoh would soon find out who the Lord is. He is the One who was going to set Israel free, totally defeating her conquerors. He is the same God, with all His miracle-working power, who rescued Israel, and did so with a high and mighty hand. He is the same God you are serving today. He has not changed. To be sure, He has revealed Himself in an even greater way in the presentation of His only Son and our Saviour, the Lord Jesus Christ.

Pharaoh's response to the overtures of God's grace is recorded in this verse. Unacquainted with God himself, he defiantly refused to bow to His mandate. Consequently, the character of Egypt's king stands fully revealed: *"I know not the LORD, neither will I let Israel go."*

THE GOSPEL

In a sense, untold millions answer God presently in the same manner as did Pharaoh. The mandate from heaven is, *"Repent! Believe!"*

Oftentimes we speak of the gospel as an invitation. In a sense, it is, but it is more than that. It is rather a declaration of what God demands from the sinner — yes, I said demands — God *"now commands all men everywhere to repent"* (Acts 17:30). It should be obvious, true prophets and true evangelists do not deliver a diplomatic word, but rather an ultimatum. However, the response of the natural man all too often is, *"Who is the Lord that I should obey His voice?"* Thus speaks the pride of the man who hardens his neck against the blessed God.

Pharaoh bluntly thundered, *"I know Him not,"* and those same words express the heart of much of the world presently.

What makes it even worse, ignorant men seem to have no desire to correct this ignorance. They do not know, and if they did know, they would not believe that one day soon, God will be revealed *"in flaming fire taking vengeance on them who know not God, and who obey not the gospel of our Lord Jesus Christ"* (II Thess. 1:8).

SACRIFICE

"And they said, The God of the Hebrews has met with us: let us go, we pray you, three days' journey into the desert, and sacrifice unto the LORD our God; lest He fall upon us with pestilence, or with the sword" (Ex. 5:3).

If attention is called to the practice, we find that sacrifice had been practiced from the time of the fall in the garden of Eden and was never to be set aside. The sacrifice of a clean animal, such as a lamb, a goat, a heifer, an ox, or a ram, typified the coming Redeemer who would give Himself in order to pay the terrible sin debt owed by man to God. This was God's way of restored fellowship, which brought about forgiveness of sin, and was done through the shed blood of the innocent animal. So, we have here, at the very beginning of God's demands of Pharaoh that he let Israel go, the Cross of Christ in the form of sacrifice being set forth. It hasn't changed from then until now. It is still the Cross! The Cross! The Cross!

More than likely, the children of Israel had little kept up this practice during their years of sojourn in the land of Egypt, and the very first thing that God demanded was that this practice be reinstituted. In a sense, one might say that God was demanding that Israel once again preach the Cross. Of course, that would have been terminology that they would not at all have understood, but, in reality, that's exactly what it meant.

THE POWERS OF DARKNESS

The believer must understand that our problem is more than just a wrong direction, a bad environment, we need to try harder, etc. We must know that we as believers are facing the concentrated powers of darkness, and I speak of demon spirits, fallen angels, and Satan himself. They head up the kingdom of darkness, and their business is to steal, kill, and destroy (Jn. 10:10).

Now, we know that Paul said: *"Wherefore let him who thinks he stands* (is addressed to all believers) *take heed lest he fall.* (This means to not merely fall from fellowship as some teach, but to fall from eternal salvation. This won't happen if the Cross is ever in view).

"There has no temptation taken you but such as is common to man (refers to the limitations God has placed upon Satan respecting that which he can or cannot do): *but God is faithful, who will not suffer you to be tempted above that you are able* (we have His promise; all temptation is overcome by our faith remaining constant in Christ and the Cross, which gives the power of the Holy Spirit to help us [Rom. 8:2]); *but*

will with the temptation also make a way to escape, that you may be able to bear it. (As stated, the 'way of escape' is always the Cross)" (I Cor. 10:12-13).

WHAT IS THAT WAY OF ESCAPE?

Pure and simple, as stated, it is the Cross of Christ. At the Cross Jesus atoned for all sin — past, present, and future — at least for all who will believe (Jn. 3:16). Sin presents the legal means that Satan has to hold man captive, but with all sin removed, he legally does not have any right to hold anyone captive. So, that being the case, why is it that most of the world, even believers, are, in fact, captive to Satan?

The world that doesn't know the Lord is in the shape they're in because they will not avail themselves of the opportunity paid for by Christ at Calvary's Cross. Sadly, most Christians are also in bondage to the sin nature simply because they, as well, do not avail themselves of that which our Lord has done, which gives Satan the legal means to steal, kill, and destroy.

The Cross of Christ alone is the answer, and the only answer for sin. Paul also said: *"But this Man* (this Priest, Christ Jesus), *after He had offered one sacrifice for sins forever* (speaks of the Cross), *sat down on the right hand of God* (refers to the great contrast with the priests under the Levitical system, who never sat down because their work was never completed, the work of Christ was and is a finished work, and needs no repetition)" (Heb. 10:12). To be sure, sin is the problem. Unfortunately, most of the modern church world doesn't agree with that, but it happens to be true. Let us say it again: the only answer for sin is the Cross of Christ.

To sum up what I've said, Paul also said the following, and we must understand that he was speaking by the inspiration of the Holy Spirit.

He said: *"For we wrestle not against flesh and blood* (our foes are not human; however, Satan constantly uses human beings to carry out his dirty work), *but against principalities* (rulers or beings of the highest rank and order in Satan's kingdom of darkness), *against powers* (the rank immediately below the 'principalities') *against the rulers of the darkness of this world* (those who carry out the instructions of the 'powers') *against spiritual wickedness in high places.* (This refers to demon spirits)" (Eph. 6:12).

This is the reason that the foray of the modern church into humanistic psychology is such a travesty. What the child of God is facing cannot be helped by wisdom that is sensual and devilish (James 3:15). To be sure, the wisdom of psychology is most definitely sensual and devilish.

Besides that, the Holy Spirit through the Apostle Peter said: *"According as His divine power has given unto us all things* (the Lord with large-handed generosity has given us all things) *that pertain unto life and godliness* (pertains to the fact that the Lord Jesus has given us everything we need regarding life and living), *through the knowledge of Him who has called us to glory and virtue* (the knowledge addressed here speaks of what Christ did at the Cross, which alone can provide glory and virtue)" (II Pet. 1:3).

So, when Moses faced Pharaoh, he was facing more than a man, but he was rather facing, as well, the concentrated powers of darkness. Millions today around the world are crying for help. They love God, but they do not know how to obtain victory over the powers of darkness. The Cross of Christ is the solution for that problem, and the only solution. The believer must understand, as we've already stated, just because God has said it, and most definitely He has, it doesn't mean that Satan is going to fold his tent, so to speak, and leave. In fact, he will begin to fight harder than ever, and that's what we are addressing in this chapter.

THE MODERN CHURCH

For all practical purposes, the church presently has ceased to preach the Cross. It is preaching everything else that one can imagine, supposedly to address itself to the ills of man, but not the Cross. Let the reader understand that every preacher who preaches something else other than the Cross is, in effect, preaching *"another gospel."*

Paul said: *"I marvel that you are so soon removed from Him who called you into the grace of Christ* (the Holy Spirit) *unto another gospel* (a so-called gospel which is not the Cross)."

He then said, *"Which is not another"* (Gal. 1:6–7), meaning that this other gospel will not set any captive free, will not bless anyone, and, in fact, will not save anyone.

The apostle was so strong, as it regarded this of which I say, that he also said: *"But though we, or an angel from heaven, preach any other gospel unto you than that which we have preached unto you, let him be accursed"* (Gal. 1:8). You will find that in Galatians 1:9, he, in essence, said the same thing again. That's how critical, how significant, how weighty, and how important all of this is.

THE GOSPEL

What we're speaking of here is not a side issue, but actually the main theme of the presentation of Jesus Christ to this world. This is of such importance, and I continue to speak of the Cross, that the Holy Spirit through Peter said: *"Forasmuch as you know that you were not redeemed with corruptible things, as silver and gold ... But with the precious blood of Christ, as of a lamb without blemish and without spot:*

"Who verily was foreordained before the foundation of the world, but was manifest in these last times for you" (I Pet. 1:18–20).

As should be obvious, from these passages we gather the fact that the Cross of Christ was decided upon by the Godhead (as it regards the redemption of Adam's fallen race) even before the foundation of the world. This means that God knew that man would fall even before He made man, and even before the world was brought back to a habitable state. At that time, it was the Cross that was decided upon to be the instrument and vehicle of redemption, and that means before anything else was addressed.

JUDGMENT

On that first meeting of Moses with Pharaoh, he said to the monarch that all of Israel must go three days' journey into the desert, *"And sacrifice unto the LORD our God: lest He fall upon us with pestilence, or with the sword."*

Even though Moses didn't explain this to Pharaoh, this simple statement tells us, even as given to Moses by the Lord, that it is the Cross only that holds back the judgment of God. In other words, the only thing standing between the lost sinner and the burning fires of hell is the Cross of Christ. That's the reason we are to preach the Cross, and do so in every capacity.

That doesn't mean that every single message has to be about the Cross, but it does mean that our understanding must be that the Cross is the foundation of the entirety of every doctrine. If it's not the foundation of all doctrine, then whatever doctrine is being espoused is, pure and simple, wrong doctrine.

This demand for sacrifice as stated by Moses to Pharaoh proclaimed the fact of what God's heart sought and what man's sin needed.

Back up in the first verse, it was said that they would hold a *"feast unto the Lord in the wilderness."* The feast pointed to rejoicing; the sacrifice to what makes rejoicing possible.

As well, Israel was confessedly guilty and, therefore, deserving of punishment, and the only way of escape was through an atonement being made for them. God must be placated: blood must be shed, and the divine justice must be propitiated. Only thus could God be reconciled to Israel.

To be sure, the only manner in which God can be reconciled to man today is through man's faith in Christ and what Christ did for us at the Cross. As we have said over and over in this volume, we must never separate Christ from the Cross or the Cross from Christ. It was for this very cause that Jesus Christ came into this world. John the Baptist said of Christ in the introduction of the Son of God: *"Behold the Lamb of God, which taketh away the sin of the world"* (Jn. 1:29).

If it is to be noticed, he did not first introduce Christ as the Healer, the Miracle-Worker, the Prophet, the King, etc., but rather as the Saviour, meaning that He would be the sacrifice for sin.

THREE DAYS

The *"three days' journey into the desert,"* as demanded by Moses, speaks of the interval between death and resurrection. Of course, Israel would not have understood that then, and possibly Moses didn't either, but that's exactly what it meant. It is only on a resurrection-ground, as made alive from the dead, that we can hold a feast unto the Lord! This goes forward to Romans, Chapter 6. There Paul said: *"Do you not know, that so many of us as were baptized into Jesus Christ were baptized into His death?*

"Therefore we are buried with Him by baptism into death: that like as Christ was raised up from the dead by the glory of the Father, even so we also should walk in newness of life.

"For if we have been planted together in the likeness of His death, we shall be also in the likeness of His resurrection" (Rom. 6:3–5).

Let it be understood that Paul is not speaking of water baptism in these passages. Rather, he is speaking of the death of Christ on the Cross, and of believing sinners literally being in Christ at His death, at least in the mind of God, which is all brought about by faith. In other words, when the believing sinner expresses faith in Christ, this performs the work. As well, it is the same with the Christians, even veteran Christians who have been living for the Lord for many, many years. We must continue, and I emphasize the point, to manifest faith in Christ and what He has done for us at the Cross. This alone is the means by which victory comes to the child of God and is maintained by the child of God. That's why Paul also said: *"For in Jesus Christ neither circumcision avails anything, nor uncircumcision; but faith which works by love"* (Gal. 5:6).

In this one passage in Galatians, Paul is telling believers that it's not *works* which we perform that give us victory, but rather *faith*. Every time Paul speaks of faith, always and without exception, he is speaking of faith in Christ and what Christ did for us at the Cross (I Cor. 1:17).

THE MESSAGE

Such was Jehovah's message to Pharaoh. He claimed full deliverance for the people on the grounds of their being His and, thereby, their right and obligation to offer sacrifice unto

Him. This means that nothing could ever satisfy God in reference to His elect but their entire emancipation from the yoke of bondage.

When we contemplate Israel amid the brick kilns of Egypt, we behold a graphic condition of every child of Adam by nature, and even, regrettably, many Christians who do not know their place and position in Christ. There they were, crushed beneath the enemy's galling yoke, and having no power to deliver themselves.

As we read between the lines, we find that the mere mention of the word *liberty* only caused the oppressor to bind his captives with a stronger fetter, and to laden them with a still more grievous burden. Consequently, it was absolutely necessary that deliverance should come from without.

DELIVERANCE

From where could such deliverance come? Where were the resources to pay such a ransom? Where was the power to break their chains? Even if there were both the one and other, where was the *will*? Who would take the trouble of delivering them?

The answer to that dilemma, which holds just as true presently as it did then, was God! Their refuge was in God then, just as it is in God now! God has both the power and the will. He can accomplish a redemption both by price and by power. In Jehovah, and in Him alone, was there salvation for ruined and oppressed Israel. Thus it is in every case.

"Neither is there salvation in any other: for there is none other name under heaven given among men, whereby we must be saved" (Acts 4:12).

The sinner is in the hands of one who rules him with despotic power. He is sold under sin—led captive by Satan at his will—fast bound in the fetters of lust, passion, and temper. Without strength. Without hope. Without God.

THE VERY NATURE OF THE UNREDEEMED

It is not merely a question of the sinner's condition; his very nature is radically corrupt — wholly under the power of Satan. Hence, he not only needs to be introduced into a new condition, but also to be endowed with a new nature. In fact, the nature and the condition go together. If it were possible for the sinner to better his condition, what would it avail so long as his nature was irrecoverably bad? There must be a nature to suit the condition, and there must be a condition to suit the capacity, the desires, the affections, and the tendencies of the new nature.

THE GOSPEL OF THE GRACE OF GOD

There is only one answer to man's condition, and that is Christ and the Cross. In fact, Christ and the Cross constitute the gospel (I Cor. 1:17).

In this great and glorious gospel, this gospel of the grace of God, we are taught that the believer is introduced into an entirely new condition, which is brought about by the born-again experience. His condition is so new that he is no longer viewed as in his former state of guilt and condemnation, but as in a state of perfect and everlasting justification. It is a state of full pardon, so full, in fact, that infinite holiness cannot so much as find a single stain. This is brought about solely by the blood of Jesus Christ (Eph. 2:13–18) and, in fact, can be brought about in no other way or manner. The sinner is placed into an absolute and eternal state of a new condition of unspotted righteousness.

NO SUCH THING AS MORAL EVOLUTION

Now, please note the following and note it carefully: It is not, by any means, that his old condition is improved, for that's exactly what the world attempts to do. This is utterly impossible. *"That which is crooked cannot be made straight"* (Eccl. 1:15). And, as Jeremiah would ask, *"Can the Ethiopian change his skin, or the leopard his spots?"* (Jer. 13:23).

Nothing can be more opposed to the fundamental truth of the gospel than the theory of a gradual improvement in the sinner's condition, which, as should be obvious, completely blows to pieces the hypothesis of humanistic psychology. The sinner is born in a certain condition, and until he is born again, he cannot be in any other condition. He may try to improve, and he may resolve to be better for the future — to turn over a new leaf — to live a different sort of life, but all the while, he has not moved a single hair's breadth out of his real condition as a sinner. He may become religious, as it is called. He may try to pray, or he may diligently attend to some ordinances and exhibit an appearance of moral reform, but none of these things can, in the smallest degree, affect his negative condition before God.

NATURE

Think about this for a moment: How can a man alter his nature? He may make it undergo a process, or he may try to subdue it—to place it under discipline, which is the way of psychology—but it is a nature still. *"That which is born of the flesh is flesh"* (Jn. 3:6).

For there to be a change in the human being, there must be the insertion of a new nature as well as a new condition. How is this to be had?

It is to be had only by believing God's testimony concerning His Son.

"As many as received Him, to them gave He power to become the sons of God, even to them who believe on His name:

"Which were born, not of blood, nor of the will of the flesh, nor of the will of man, but of God" (Jn. 1:12–13).

Here we learn that those who believe on the name of the only begotten Son of God have the right and privilege of being sons of God. They are made partakers of a new nature: they have received eternal life. *"He who believes on the Son has everlasting life"* (Jn. 3:36).

Jesus said: *"Verily, verily, I say unto you, He who 'hears' My Word, and 'believes' on Him who sent Me, 'has' everlasting life, and shall not come into condemnation; but is passed from death unto life"* (Jn. 5:24).

CONDITION AND NATURE

Such is the plain doctrine of the Word in reference to the momentous questions of condition and nature, but on what is all this founded? How is the believer introduced into a condition of divine righteousness and made partaker of the divine nature?

It all rests on the great truth that *"Jesus died and rose again."* He died on the Cross under the full weight of the transgressions of all of mankind. By so doing, He divinely met all that was or could be against us. He magnified the law by keeping it perfectly and, thereby, made it honorable. Having done so, He was made a curse, as well, by being placed on the tree. There, every claim was met, and every enemy was silenced. There, every obstacle was removed, and *"mercy and truth are met together; righteousness and peace have kissed each other."*

There, infinite justice was satisfied. There, infinite love could once again flow in all its soothing and refreshing virtues, even into the broken heart of the sinner. There, the cleansing and atoning stream that flowed from the pierced side of a crucified Christ perfectly met all the cravings of a guilty and convicted conscience. There, the Lord Jesus, on the Cross, stood in our place, and there, He was our representative. There, He died, *"the just for the unjust."* There, He was made sin for us (I Pet. 3:18; II Cor. 5:21). There, He died the sinner's death, was buried, and rose again, having accomplished all. Hence, there is absolutely nothing now against the believer. He is linked with Christ and stands now in the same condition of righteousness. *"As He is, so are we in this world"* (I Jn. 4:17).

This is so important that we must say it again: There, and we continue to speak of the Cross, the blood of the Lamb has canceled all the believer's guilt. There, Jesus blotted out the sinner's heavy debt. There, Christ gave to all who will believe a perfectly blank page, meaning that all the sins have been washed away.

THE CROSS

In all of this, we find that the Cross must be viewed in two ways:

1. As satisfying God's claims.
2. As expressing God's affections.

If I look at my sins in connection with the claims of God as a judge, I find in the Cross a perfect settlement of those claims. God, as a judge, has been divinely satisfied — yes, glorified, in the Cross, but there is more than this.

God has affections as well as claims. In the Cross of the Lord Jesus Christ, all of those affections are sweetly and touchingly told out into the sinner's ear. At the same time, he is made partaker of a new nature that is capable of enjoying those affections and having fellowship with a heart from which they flow. *"For Christ also has once suffered for sins, the just for the unjust, that He might bring us to God"* (I Pet. 3:18).

Thus, we are not only brought into a *condition*, but unto a *person*, even God Himself, and we are endowed with a nature that can delight in Him. The Scripture says, *"We also joy in God through our Lord Jesus Christ, by whom we now have received the atonement* (reconciliation)*"* (Rom. 5:11).

THE BELIEVER AND THE CROSS

Everything we have said thus far speaks of the sinner coming to Christ and the tremendous change that takes place in his life. It is a change that is so drastic, in fact, that he is now referred to as a *"new creation,"* all in Christ Jesus (II Cor. 5:17). Unfortunately, unless the believer is taught how to live for God, the new life that has been imparted to him can be hindered and weakened, causing failure, consternation, and acute difficulty in such a believer. Sadly, most believers fall into this situation simply because they are taught incorrectly once they come to Christ.

The believer must understand that this which brought him eternal life, and we continue to speak of Christ and the Cross, is that, as well, which maintains eternal life. In other words, the way the believer is to live a victorious, overcoming, Christian life — which Peter said is *"joy unspeakable and full of glory"* — is to continue to look to the Cross. He must understand that it is through the Cross that the grace of God continues to flow to the believer.

Each and every believer is meant to live under the government of grace, but unfortunately, many have fallen back to the government of law.

THE GOVERNMENT OF GRACE

Let us explain: Paul said, *"For you are not under the law* (the government of law), *but under grace* (the government of grace)" (Rom. 6:14).

This refers not only to the dispensation under which we now live, which began at the Cross of Christ, but, as well, it refers to the *way* and *manner* in which we live and conduct ourselves. What do we mean by that?

Many Christians erroneously think that because this is the dispensation of grace, and to be sure it definitely is, this means that we are no longer troubled by law. They consider that due to the fact that this is the dispensation of grace, this grace just automatically comes to them. It doesn't!

It is possible to frustrate the grace of God, and to do so to the extent that we stop, or at least seriously hinder, its flow, irrespective of the fact that we are living in the dispensation of grace (Gal. 2:21).

The believer must understand that the dispensation or government of grace simply refers to the manner in which God deals with the human race. He deals with it in grace simply because the Cross has made this possible.

GRACE AND SIN

Now, grace doesn't mean that we have a license to sin, as some think, but rather that the goodness of God, which is what grace actually is, will flow to us in an uninterrupted stream, so to speak, because of what Jesus did for us at the Cross. In other words, the grace of God is tied indivisibly to the Cross; therefore, it troubles me greatly when I hear Christians refer to *"greasy grace"* or *"easy grace."* Pure and simple, these individuals, whomever they might be, are functioning under the government of law. In fact, they are despising grace because it sets aside the government of law.

There is no such thing as greasy grace or easy grace. Such people who say these things are, in effect, despising grace, claiming that it gives people a license to sin. In fact, the exact opposite is the truth.

It is by the grace of God, which is the goodness of God, that we are given total and complete victory over sin. It is all brought about by what Jesus did at the Cross, which gives the Holy Spirit the latitude to work within our lives. Now, we aren't speaking of sinless perfection because the Bible doesn't teach such. However, we are speaking of the fact that if our faith is in Christ and the Cross, then sin will not have dominion over us (Rom. 6:14). The Cross of Christ gives the Holy Spirit latitude to work within our lives, at least if our faith is anchored squarely in Christ and the Cross.

This which Paul taught, and which we are teaching, is the way to have victory over sin and, in fact, the only way to have victory over sin. If anyone tries to do it any other way, that person, whether he realizes it or not, is repudiating the Cross of Christ, which can only play out to a disastrous conclusion.

GOVERNMENT?

What do we mean by the term *government of grace?*

In simple explanation, we are referring to the fact that the believer understands that everything comes to him through Christ and what Christ did for us at the Cross. He is to continue to believe in that finished work, which then enables the grace of God to come to him in an uninterrupted flow. All it takes is faith, and when we speak of faith, as always, we're speaking of Christ and His finished work. That's why Paul said, *"For in Jesus Christ neither circumcision availeth anything, nor uncircumcision; but faith which worketh by love"* (Gal. 5:6).

This, the government of grace, is God's prescribed order for victorious, Christian living. As long as the believer continues to manifest faith in Christ and the Cross, grace will always come to him in an uninterrupted flow, which actually refers to the Holy Spirit working unhindered within his heart and life.

THE GOVERNMENT OF LAW

This particular type of government rested on Israel for a period of about 1,600 years. It was given to Moses and was concluded by Jesus Christ. John said, *"For the law was given by Moses, but grace and truth came by Jesus Christ"* (Jn. 1:17).

The Cross of Christ introduced a completely new manner of living. The deity of Christ was absolutely necessary; however, not a single soul has ever been saved because Christ was and is God. In other words, the fact of Jesus being deity could not save anyone. As well, the virgin birth was absolutely necessary; however, the virgin birth within itself could not save one single soul. Jesus' perfect life was absolutely necessary, but had it stopped there, not one soul would have been saved. His miracles were necessary, but the miracles and healings alone could not save anyone.

THE CROSS ALONE

It was the Cross alone, which is the atonement and is where Christ shed His precious life's blood, that satisfied the demands of a thrice-holy God and, thereby, atoned for all sin and effected salvation. Jesus' perfect life means that He kept the law in every respect. As well, His perfect death, which refers to Him offering up His perfect body as a perfect sacrifice, atoned for all sin. It was an absolute necessity if the terrible sin debt was to be paid, and man could be saved. So, the law was satisfied by Christ in two ways:

1. It was perfectly kept, which Jesus did as our substitute.
2. Its penalty was perfectly met, which also was demanded, and which took place at the Cross.

All the precepts of the law were perfectly kept by Christ, and all the conditions of the law were perfectly met by Christ. Concerning this, Paul also said: *"Blotting out the handwriting of ordinances that was against us* (the law), *which was contrary to us, and took it out of the way, nailing it to His Cross"* (Col. 2:14). This means that Jesus met every condition of the law and did so all on our behalf.

SIN

Sin is what breaks the law, and sin is the legal means by which Satan holds man in bondage. However, when Jesus died on the Cross, He atoned for all sin. When He did this, which means that all sin was removed, this *"spoiled principalities and powers ... made a show of them openly, triumphing over them in it"* (Col. 2:15).

This means that Satan was totally defeated, along with every fallen angel and demon spirit. This also means that Satan can no longer hold man in bondage, at least those who will believe in Christ and what Christ has done at the Cross.

Because this is the dispensation of grace, many Christians think it's impossible for one to revert to law. In fact, most Christians have little knowledge of what the law is all about. The tragedy is, most Christians who think this way are, in fact, living under the government of law whether they realize it or not. This is proven by the constant failure within their hearts and lives. Please remember, the Christian only has two alternatives, and that is grace and law. To be sure, every believer is in one of these particular governments, so to speak.

PAUL AND THE LAW

Why do you think that Paul talked so much about law in his epistles? If it were not possible for a Christian to revert to law, then the apostle was wasting his breath.

Listen to what he said: *"Stand fast therefore in the liberty* (government of grace) *wherewith Christ has made us free, and be not entangled again with the yoke of bondage* (he's speaking here of the law)" (Gal. 5:1).

He then said: *"Behold, I Paul say unto you, that if you be circumcised* (fall back to law), *Christ shall profit you nothing.*

"For I testify again to every man who is circumcised, that he is a debtor to do the whole law."

And then: *"Christ is become of no effect unto you, whosoever of you are justified by the law* (who seek to be justified by the law); *you are fallen from grace"* (Gal. 5:2–4).

Let us say it again: if it's not possible for the believer to revert back to law, then Paul used a lot of ink for nothing.

THE GREATEST PROBLEM IN THE CHURCH

This of which we speak — Christians living under the government of law — is the greatest problem in the church. In fact, proven by what Paul said, it is the greatest problem for all time, at least since the government of grace began.

Now, please understand, when we talk about law, we aren't necessarily talking about the law of Moses, although such is once again making great headway in the modern church. However, we are also speaking of laws that we devise ourselves, some preacher devises, some denomination devises, etc.

If you will notice carefully what Paul said, he used terms like, *"Christ shall profit you nothing"* and *"Christ is become of no effect unto you,"* which presents a chilling prospect. This is the problem in countless hearts and lives of modern Christians, in fact, almost all.

How?

Why?

If the believer doesn't understand the Cross, how it affects his everyday living before God, and how he must maintain faith in the finished work of Christ at all times (Rom. 6:3–5, 11, 14), then without fail, he will revert to the government of law. As previously stated, there are only two governments under which a person can function, and that is under law or under grace. So, if the Cross is not understood, which means that we stop the grace of God, there is no place else to go but law.

MODERN PRACTICES

Let's look a little closer at the modern scene. Everything I'm about to say proves that such Christians, as sincere as they might be, are living under the government of law and not under grace.

Because it is so important, let us say it again: If the believer doesn't understand the Cross as it refers to his sanctification, this means that he doesn't understand grace. Whether he realizes it or not, he is functioning, or trying to do so, under law. As such, he will live a life of failure simply because the Holy Spirit will not help such a Christian. This means that such a believer is left to his own strength, which is hopelessly inadequate. As I explained to you some pages back, in the eyes of God, such a Christian is actually looked at as a spiritual adulterer. It means that while he is married to Christ, he is being unfaithful to Him by being married to the law as well (Rom. 7:1–4).

This is a miserable existence for a Christian. That's why Paul said: *"O wretched man that I am! who shall deliver me from the body of this death?"* (Rom. 7:24).

Paul was saved and baptized with the Holy Spirit, but he did not know or understand the Cross at that time, or grace for that matter. Therefore, for a period of time, the great apostle attempted to live for God under the government of law, which was all he knew. In his defense, no one else at that time knew and understood the government of grace. In fact, it was to Paul that the meaning of this great government was given, which he gave to us in his 14 epistles. Jesus Christ is the new covenant, and the Cross is the meaning of this new covenant, the meaning of which was given to Paul by our Lord.

Regrettably, most Christians presently are living in Chapter 7 of Romans simply because they don't know any better. Now, let's look at the practices.

ERRONEOUS PRACTICES

Millions of Christians, who are having problems and troubles within their Christian experience, are running all over the world, trying to find a preacher who will lay hands on them and solve their problems. While the laying on of hands is definitely scriptural, the manner in which it is usually performed will, in fact, bring no relief whatsoever.

The Spirit of God definitely moves in such cases, with great manifestations taking place at times that are of God. Still, when the Christian leaves that place of blessing and goes back out to his regular and normal living, he will find himself in the same condition as he was before the blessing. Why?

Jesus said, *"You shall know the truth, and the truth shall make you free"* (Jn. 8:32). This means that it's not a touch that is so much needed, but rather the truth.

The reason that such a believer continues to have problems, even after the Lord has manifested Himself to that believer, is because the believer doesn't know in the first place why he's having problems, and doesn't know the cure for those problems. As a result, there is no way that he can overcome that which He seeks to overcome.

His need is not for a preacher to lay hands on him because that's not God's way. His need is to know and understand the truth and apply it, thereby, to his heart and life. What is that truth?

Notice again what Paul said: *"For Christ sent me not to baptize, but to preach the gospel: not with wisdom of words, lest the Cross of Christ should be made of none effect.*

"For the preaching of the Cross is to them who perish foolishness; but unto us which are saved it is the power of God" (I Cor. 1:17–18).

Notice again: *"But God forbid that I should glory, save in the Cross of our Lord Jesus Christ, by whom the world is crucified unto me, and I unto the world"* (Gal. 6:14).

Every Christian in the world who is having problems can have those problems solved by understanding what we are teaching here. I speak of an understanding of the Cross and what Christ there did for us as our substitute. Our salvation was brought about by what Christ did at the Cross. Our continued victory in this salvation, which refers to living an overcoming, victorious life, is maintained by continuing to have faith in Christ and His finished work. Notice what John the Beloved said: *"For whatsoever is born of God overcomes the world, and this is the victory that overcomes the world, even our faith"* (I Jn. 5:4).

FAITH

When John speaks here of faith, even as Paul, he is speaking of Christ and what Christ did at the Cross.

Notice again what he said: *"This is He who came by water and blood, even Jesus Christ; not by water only, but by water and blood"* (I Jn. 5:6).

The *water* refers to the incarnation. In other words, it refers to Jesus being born as a human being by and through the Virgin Mary.

Blood refers to what He did to redeem the human race, which is the reason He came. He died on the Cross, thereby, shedding His life's blood, which atoned for all sin — past, present, and future — at least for those who will believe (Jn. 3:16).

I have preached the gospel now a little over a half century. During these many years, I have seen many things in the realm of Christendom, and I speak of ways that Christians engage in order to live an overcoming life.

When Frances and I first began in the ministry, the great craze then was *"casting demons out of Christians,"* etc. This referred to Christians who had problems, with these problems being diagnosed as a demon of lust, a demon of greed, or whatever it might be. They were encouraged to go to preachers who believed this, where hands would be laid on them and this particular demon or demons cast out of them. Their problems would then be solved. Pure and simple, all of that is unscriptural.

CONFESSION

I then watched the *"confession craze"* as it began in the church. The way to overcome was to simply confess, and to do so over and over again, whatever the need was and whatever the believer hoped to be. That swept through the church like wildfire and is unscriptural as well.

Now, as we go down through these things, if the believer will think a moment, he will realize that there is some truth in all of these situations. Of course, that is one of Satan's chief ploys. He puts a little truth into the situation in order to serve as bait.

For instance, demon spirits definitely do get involved wherever sin occasions itself, but the proposed solution is definitely not the answer. Also, a good and proper confession is definitely right and scriptural, but not in the manner in which it was taught.

THE BUDDY SYSTEM

I then watched the *"buddy system"* take hold, which is really a take-off on humanistic psychology. In other words, certain preachers were advocating that every believer should have a confidant. To this other person, we would confess all of our problems, with the idea being that the strength of two is far greater than the strength of one. Again, there is a small measure of truth in this, but neither is that the answer.

FALLING OUT

I then watched the *"falling out"* craze take effect, which seems to be with us constantly. In other words, if hands could be laid on the individual, as we mentioned some paragraphs back, with the person *"falling out under the power,"* this person's problems were then solved. While we definitely believe in the laying on of hands, and while falling out under the power is definitely of the Lord, that is, if He is the One truly doing such, still, this is not an answer for the ills of man.

When that person gets up, unless he knows the truth, he's going to go right back into the same problem.

THE LAUGHING PHENOMENON

In the early 1990s, the *"laughing phenomenon"* took hold in the church. It was advised that if everyone could have the Spirit of God move on them, thereby, engaging in peals of laughter for a given period of time, this would bring about victory. Again, this is not scriptural.

THE FAMILY CURSE

Then, we have the *"family curse,"* which claims that certain preachers can lay hands on people, rebuke the family curse, and victory will then join itself to that particular believer.

They teach that if one's great-great grandfather, or some such like, did something terrible in years past, this means the person was cursed by God, and the curse would pass down several generations.

Of course, the question must be asked, *"Is there such a thing as a family curse?"*

Most definitely there is! In fact, there are all types of curses on the unredeemed: the family curse, the generational curse, the curse of the broken law, etc. However, whenever the believing sinner comes to Christ and is born again, every single curse is broken.

Paul said: *"Christ has redeemed us from the curse of the law, being made a curse for us: for it is written, Cursed is every one who hangs on a tree"* (Gal. 3:13). So, no believer need ever have to worry about having some curse hanging over his or her head.

In fact, claiming that a family curse exists in the hearts and lives of Christians, in effect, is stating that what Jesus did at the Cross is not enough, and other things have to be added. Actually, this borders on blasphemy. The Cross answered the curse, and did so in every capacity.

FASTING

Many preachers have concluded that if a person wants victory over sin, then he must go on a 21-day fast, a 10-day fast, a 40-day fast, or whatever it is they suggest.

Once again, while fasting is definitely scriptural and will bless the individual, at least if it's done in the right way, fasting is not an answer for the sin problem, and to be sure, the problem is sin. In fact, when we believe such, we have just turned fasting into a law.

Look what Paul said about this: *"I am crucified with Christ: nevertheless I live; yet not I, but Christ lives in me: and the life which I now live in the flesh I live by the faith of the Son of God, who loved me, and gave Himself for me.*

"I do not frustrate the grace of God: for if righteousness come by the law, then Christ is dead in vain" (Gal. 2:20-21).

These things, and scores we haven't named, have no validity, scripturally speaking. The reason is, the Lord doesn't deliver people by and through manifestations or particular works. People are delivered by faith, and by that, we are speaking of faith in Christ and what Christ has done for us at the Cross. That and that alone is the answer. Again I emphasize, that's why Jesus said, *"You shall know the truth, and the truth shall make you free"* (Jn. 8:32).

ABANDONING THE CROSS

All of this is what I mean by Christians abandoning the Cross and resorting to other things, which automatically places them under the government of law. When this happens, even as Paul said, *"Christ then profits them nothing,"* which means that what He did at the Cross has become of no effect (Gal. 5:2, 4).

People who live under the government of law have placed their faith in works, which then has to do with their performance, which is always lacking.

Let the reader understand this as well: One cannot trust in Christ and what Christ has done for us in His finished work and, at the same time, trust in works. Such proclaims a double-minded man, which the Holy Spirit through James told us *"is unstable in all his ways."* He also said of such a man, *"For let not that man think that he shall receive anything of the Lord"* (James 1:7–8).

THE MESSAGE OF THE CROSS

Anytime the Christian answers the Message of the Cross by saying, *"I believe that, but ..."* the truth is, that Christian doesn't believe it. In other words, he is paying lip service, if that, to the Cross, with his faith actually being anchored in his own concoction, whatever that might be.

Sometime back, one of my very close associates was speaking with a preacher about this very thing. The man pastored a quite large church in a major American city.

To the Message of the Cross, the preacher answered, *"That's alright for some people, but not necessarily for all."*

What in the world type of answer is that? What in the world could a man mean by such an answer?

Whether he realized it or not, he was saying that the Cross of Christ was needed for some but not for all. What is that man preaching to his congregation?

The tragedy is, this very preacher was found out just a little later to be suffering a tremendous problem within his life, which was threatening to destroy him and, in fact, did. And yet, as he answered my associate, he was, in effect, putting himself in the position as not needing the Cross, despite his problem that he had been struggling for years to try to overcome.

I think we are speaking here of pride, which seems to affect all of us, and which is a fallout from the problem in the garden.

PRIDE

Pride is very bad, and religious pride is the worst pride of all. It refuses to admit its need or its condition. Why?

Such a person is trying to live for God under the government of law. As such, he has engaged himself in certain works and practices, and it's hard for him to admit that all of these things are to no avail. That's why Paul said: *"For in Jesus Christ neither circumcision availeth anything, nor uncircumcision"* (Gal. 5:6).

In effect, these Galatians were saying, *"I believe in the Cross, but I also believe that Christian men have to be circumcised."* To such a belief, the apostle said, *"Christ is become of no effect unto you, whosoever of you are justified by the law."* He then offered a chilling statement, *"You are fallen from grace"* (Gal. 5:4).

In other words, such a Christian is not functioning under the government of grace, but rather the government of law.

The only answer for the child of God, in fact, for the entirety of the world, is *"Jesus Christ and Him crucified."* To look elsewhere is to look in vain.

THE BURDENS

"And the king of Egypt said unto them, Wherefore do you, Moses and Aaron, let the people from their works? get you unto your burdens.

"And Pharaoh said, Behold, the people of the land now are many, and you make them rest from their burdens" (Ex. 5:4-5).

With the words registered in Verses 4 and 5, the first confrontation between the Israelite leaders and the Egyptian monarch ends.

The word *burdens* is apropos as it regards the condition of the children of Israel at this time. As we shall see, their lot was difficult to say the least. While we will deal with this subject of *"burdens"* to a greater degree a little later, let us touch it by saying the following: The command of the Lord has been given, *"Let My people go."* The answer of Pharaoh to that was, instead of obeying the Lord, he rather increased their burdens. In other words, he increased their workload to a killing pace.

This means that once you as a believer hear the truth about the Cross as it refers to victory within your life, you will find oftentimes, if not all the time, that Satan will increase his temptations, his pressure, and his power against you. This will confuse most Christians.

If the Message of the Cross is scriptural, many think, why is the situation now worse instead of better? It is worse because Satan knows that you have heard the truth, and if, through discouragement, he can get you to throw over the truth, then he has won the battle, and your situation is going to fall out to be worse than ever.

So, Satan increasing the pressure, which he most definitely will do, is a perfect sign that you've heard the truth. He knows that if you stay with this truth, you are going to be free; consequently, he will do everything he can to discourage you as a believer.

On the other side of the coin, so to speak, until the burden becomes so heavy that it cannot be borne, many Christians are content to remain the way they were. Please remember this: the powers of darkness never remain where they were, but the situation always gets worse and worse, with total destruction in mind.

SPIRITUAL BLINDNESS

Every unsaved person in the world is spiritually blind, and they are spiritually blind because they are spiritually dead. At the fall in the garden of Eden, man died. This means that he spiritually died, which means that all access to God was cut off because of sin. This means that the unredeemed man is totally depraved and has no idea or correct knowledge of God whatsoever. In fact, it is impossible for him to have any knowledge of God or God's Word. Dead is dead and means exactly what it says (Eph. 2:1).

So, being spiritually dead, the individual doesn't really understand the state that he's in. If he looks at Christians at all, which he oftentimes does, it is a mystery to him as to how they could reap any enjoyment out of going to church, reading the Bible, etc. In fact, he really cannot think of anything that's more boring than that which we've just stated.

Consequently, being spiritually dead, he has absolutely no knowledge of the joy of the Lord, of the peace which passes all understanding, etc. If a Christian tries to explain these things to the unredeemed, at best, he will only draw a blank stare.

Again, let us emphasize it: Being spiritually dead, man is totally depraved, which means that not only does he have no knowledge of God, neither does he have any knowledge of sin. Sin is natural to him, actually being his very nature, i.e., the sin nature.

So, Satan piles the burdens on such an individual, but he thinks that such are natural. As stated, until those burdens become insurmountable, he is not prone to turn to Christ.

THE BELIEVER AND THE POWERS OF DARKNESS

While the believer is definitely not in the state of the unbeliever, still, many Christians are content to live and let live, as it concerns Satan's efforts in their hearts and lives, as long as it doesn't come to the place of destruction. Please believe me, Satan's aim is destruction.

Despite what Pharaoh was doing to them, as we shall later see, the elders of Israel were quite willing to make a deal with the monarch if he would let up a little bit on the pressure (Ex. 5:15). Please understand, Satan is not going to let up. If he does, it will be only for a short season and with a purpose in mind of drawing you deeper into the net. He means to steal, kill, and destroy, and to do so totally (Jn. 10:10).

FREE WILL

God never tampers with the free moral agency of a person. He will deal with that person, speak to that person, move upon that person, and even convict that person by the power of the Holy Spirit, but He will not force the issue. God always respects the free will of an individual. As stated, it is *"whosoever will"* (Rev. 22:17; Jn. 3:16).

Of course, God through foreknowledge knows who will accept and who will reject, but foreknowledge doesn't at all mean that God tampers with the will. It just simply means that He foreknows through His omniscience what is going to happen in the future. However, let me explain something about the will of man that most people do not know or realize.

The will of an individual, as it regards spiritual things, is limited to the will to follow the Lord or to reject the Lord.

For instance: If the worst alcoholic in the world desires to do so as the Holy Spirit moves upon his heart, he can accept the Lord, and all the powers of darkness cannot stop him. He doesn't have the will to quit drinking or committing a myriad of other sins, but Satan is not allowed to stop his will as it regards accepting Christ, that is, if he *wills* to do so. It is still *"whosoever will."* Of course, after turning to Christ, as millions have in this state, the Holy Spirit then rids that person of the demon spirits that are controlling him and gives him, as well, victory over sin.

A WRONG VIEWPOINT

Strangely enough, many, if not most, Christians have an erroneous viewpoint of the will of the believer. Most think that once they come to Christ, their willpower is greatly strengthened, and now they have the power to do what they didn't have the power to do before being saved, and that is to say no to sin. Nothing could be further from the truth.

In effect, the will of man, as it regards the Lord, is the same in the believer as it is the unbeliever. By that, I mean the believer has the will to say yes to Christ, and at the same time, if he so desires, he can also say no exactly as the unredeemed. The Lord doesn't strengthen the willpower of the believer, as many think. In fact, even though the will is always very much involved in what the believer does, and he definitely has to *will* to have all that Christ has afforded him, that's as far as it goes. No Christian has any super willpower or anything like that.

I had a dear brother say to me not long ago, *"Before I was saved, I couldn't say no to drugs. But now that I'm saved, I can say no to that terrible scourge."*

That dear brother has been taught wrong, and following that particular course, he will find himself in trouble very shortly if, in fact, that trouble hasn't already come by now.

SO, HOW DOES THE CHRISTIAN WALK IN VICTORY?

Exactly as the unsaved has the capacity to use his will to accept Christ, the believer has the same identical capacity.

He is to *will* to go God's way, which means the way of the Cross, thereby, placing his faith in that finished work. This then gives the Holy Spirit the latitude to work mightily in that believer's life. There is no place in the Scripture where it says that it is by the will of the believer, but rather by faith.

The will is important only as a means of desiring that which is of the Lord. That's as far as it can go. Having done that, we are to will to register faith in Christ and what Christ has done for us at the Cross. That and that alone brings victory.

Listen again to Paul: *"For I know that in me (that is, in my flesh,) dwells no good thing: for to will is present with me; but how to perform that which is good I find not"* (Rom. 7:18).

Paul plainly says here that he had the will, but that simply wasn't enough. He was to later find out that it was faith in Christ and what Christ has done for us at the Cross that brings about victory in one's life.

Unfortunately, most Christians think that it is willpower that is the source of the Christian's strength. It isn't!

SATAN OVERRIDING THE WILL OF THE BELIEVER

This comes as a shock to most Christians, but Satan can override a believer's will. He does this millions of times each and every day all over the world, forcing that believer to do something he or she doesn't want to do. Once again, let's quote the passage we have just given you by Paul: *"For I know that in me (that is, in my flesh) dwells no good thing:*

for to will is present with me; but how to perform that which is good I find not" (Rom. 7:18).

So, if the believer is trying to live for God by the means of willpower alone, he will find Satan overriding his will and forcing him into a situation to which he has no desire to go but is unable to stop himself. As stated, it is happening millions of times every day.

Most Christians are trying to live for God by the means of willpower, which is impossible.

Listen again to Paul: *"For I delight in the law of God after the inward man:*

"But I see another law in my members, warring against the law of my mind (this is the law of desire and willpower), *and bringing me into captivity to the law of sin which is in my members"* (Rom. 7:22-23).

In other words, every single believer in the world hates sin. While the flesh at times may want something that's wrong, the inward man doesn't. We are now new creations in Christ, and sin is abhorrent to any believer. So, if that is the case, and it definitely is, then why is it that Christians sin?

As stated, most Christians are trying to ward off Satan by their willpower, which is woefully inadequate. As we've already stated, while the will is definitely important, it alone is not enough.

For the believer to overcome the powers of darkness, the Holy Spirit has to enter the scene and has to do the doing. What is impossible for us is totally possible for Him, considering that the Holy Spirit is God and can do anything.

So, how do I get the Holy Spirit to work within my heart and life?

HOW THE HOLY SPIRIT WORKS

It is the Cross of Christ that gives the Holy Spirit the legal means to do all that He does. For instance, before the Cross, due to the fact that the blood of bulls and goats could not take away sins (Heb. 10:4), this meant the sin debt remained in the believer. That being the case, the Holy Spirit could come into the hearts and lives of certain ones, such as prophets, and help them perform their tasks. When that was done, He would leave. As it regarded all other believers, while He was with them, He was not in them. That's what Jesus was talking about when He said: *"For He dwells with you, and shall be in you"* (Jn. 14:17). In fact, when believers died before the Cross, their souls and spirits could not go to heaven at that time, once again, because animal blood was insufficient to take away the sin debt.

So, they were taken down into paradise, where they were actually captives of Satan. While he could not hurt them, and, in fact, they were comforted, still, their total salvation awaited the Cross. That's what Paul meant when he said, concerning Jesus going down into this place after His crucifixion, *"He led captivity captive"* (Eph. 4:8). This means that Jesus made all the people in paradise His captives, which included everyone who was saved up until the time of the Cross. In other words, they were no longer captives of Satan. The sin debt had been paid. Ever since the Cross, when a believer dies, the soul and the spirit of such a person instantly go to be with the Lord Jesus Christ in heaven (Phil. 1:23).

Now, due to the Cross, which paid the terrible sin debt in full, at the conversion of the believing sinner, the Holy Spirit comes into the heart and life to stay, and to stay forever (Jn. 14:16).

The Holy Spirit now lives within our hearts and lives, and does so permanently. Knowing that He is God, which means that He can do anything, how do we open the door to Him that He work within our lives, helping us to overcome the world, the flesh, and the Devil?

We must understand that the way the Holy Spirit works is not some automatic process. Stop and think a moment. If He just automatically worked, there would not be a single failure among a single Christian. However, we know that's not true, don't we?

It is the Cross of Christ that gave and gives the Holy Spirit the latitude to work within our lives.

Listen to Paul: *"For the law of the Spirit of life in Christ Jesus has made me free from the law of sin and death"* (Rom. 8:2).

Understanding this, it is imperative that our faith be exclusively in Christ and the Cross and not other things. The Cross of Christ, as we have repeatedly stated, is the means by which all things come to us by the Lord Jesus Christ. While Christ is the source, it is the Holy Spirit who actually does the doing.

If the believer will place his faith exclusively in Christ and the Cross, and maintain it exclusively in Christ and the Cross, the Holy Spirit will work mightily on our behalf, giving us victory over Satan and all of his demons.

SPIRITUAL ADULTERY

If the believer, however, places his or her faith in something other than Christ and the Cross, and it makes no difference whatever the other is or how scriptural it might be in its own way, still, the Lord will not honor such. For instance, as previously stated, there are many preachers who claim that if the believer will fast 21 days, or some such number, that will give him victory over sin. While fasting is scriptural and important, it will not give one victory over sin. It is the Cross and the Cross alone that gives us the victory. That's where our faith must be anchored. If we're placing our faith elsewhere, we are being unfaithful to Christ, and the Holy Spirit refers to such as spiritual adultery (Rom. 7:1-4). To be sure, the Holy Spirit is not going to help somebody to sin, and faith placed anywhere except Christ and the Cross is sin (Rom. 14:23). Now, let us say this again because it's so very important.

When the believer places his or her faith in something other than Christ and the Cross, no matter how viable the other thing might be, the Holy Spirit looks at that as being unfaithful to Christ and, thereby, the believer committing spiritual adultery. To be sure, the Holy Spirit is not going to help someone in that state. He doesn't demand a lot of us, but He does demand one thing, and that is that our faith be exclusively in Christ and what Christ has done for us at the Cross. Then He will work mightily on our behalf (Rom. 6:1-14; 8:1-11; I Cor. 1:17, 18, 23; 2:2; Col. 2:10-15).

SO, HOW DOES THE CHRISTIAN WALK IN VICTORY?

Actually, we've already answered that question, but let us briefly allude to it again.

All victory for the child of God is found in the Cross of Christ, and I mean all victory. The Cross is where Satan was defeated, plus all his minions of darkness (Col. 2:14-15).

The believer is to understand that and act upon it. We are to understand that Jesus Christ is the source of all things that we receive from God. The Cross is the means by which all of these things are done, in which the Holy Spirit, as stated, works. So, if the believer will place his or her faith exclusively in Christ and the Cross, understanding that the Cross of Christ is the means, and the only means by which all of these wonderful things are given to us, the Holy Spirit will then guarantee victory for the child of God. That doesn't mean sinless perfection, for the Bible does not teach such, but it does mean that sin will not have dominion over us (Rom. 6:14).

Unfortunately, and also as previously stated, most Christians are trying to live for God by the means of willpower. They think that since they have come to Christ, the Lord gives them some type of super will. None of that is true. While the will is important, it alone is incapable of bringing us to the place we ought to be.

We are to live for God not by the means of willpower, but by the means of faith; however, the faith of which the Bible speaks is faith in Christ and what He did for us at the Cross.

SIN AND THE CHRISTIAN

Before coming to Christ, every unredeemed person has a *human nature* and, as well, a *sin nature.* The sin nature came about at the fall and actually is the cause of all the suffering and heartache in the world today and, in fact, ever has been. When that person comes to Christ, he now adds a third nature, which Peter calls the *"divine nature"* (II Pet. 1:4). The sin nature has had its power destroyed and its guilt removed (Rom. 6:6). However, it does not leave the believer, as Paul explains in Romans, Chapter 6, but is rather dormant in the believer's life. In fact, the Scripture plainly tells us that we as believers are to be *dead* to the sin nature, but it doesn't say that the sin nature itself is dead (Rom. 6:11).

At any rate, due to the divine nature now being a part of the child of God, the Christian hates sin. This means that he doesn't want to sin, doesn't desire to sin, will struggle against sin, etc. So, that being the case, why is it that Christians, at times, sin?

In fact, all Christians, at times, sin, and when it happens, the true believer cannot rest until he makes it right with God. Fellowship is then restored, which means that all is forgiven (I Jn. 1:9).

OUR PLACE AND POSITION IN CHRIST

Christians sin because they do not understand their rightful place and position in Christ as a result of what Christ did at the Cross. Not understanding the Message of the Cross, which is the only message of victory, most Christians put their faith in something other than the Cross. This denies that person the help of the Holy Spirit, which guarantees failure on the part of the child of God. Now, don't misunderstand, the Holy Spirit will do all that He can do under such circumstances, but to be sure, with the believer going in the wrong direction, in other words, placing his or her faith in something other than Christ and the Cross, this greatly hinders the Holy Spirit. In fact, it just about guarantees failure on the part of the child of God. Even as we've already explained in this volume, if the Christian doesn't understand the Cross, he can find himself being ruled by the sin nature exactly as he was before conversion.

Paul said so: *"Let not sin* (the sin nature) *therefore reign in your mortal body, that you should obey it in the lusts thereof"* (Rom. 6:12).

When Paul originally wrote his epistles, many times in front of the word sin, he would write *"the sin,"* meaning that he wasn't speaking of acts of sin, but rather the root cause of sin, i.e., the sin nature. So, he actually said in the passage just quoted, *"Let not the sin,"* which refers to the definite article. In fact, in Chapter 6 of Romans, sin is mentioned some 17 times. Some 15 of those times, the apostle originally placed the definite article in front of the word sin, making it read *"the sin,"* and for the reason we have just given. The King James people did not enclose the definite article because, in some way, it makes it seem clumsy in English. At any rate, when Paul used the definite article, he was always speaking of the principle of sin instead of the acts of sin.

THE SIN NATURE

Now, if it weren't possible for the sin nature to once again rule and reign in the believer's life, then the apostle would not have mentioned it in this fashion. If such is not possible, there's no point in even bringing up the subject. However, the truth is, if the believer doesn't understand Christ and the Cross, which Paul is teaching in Romans, Chapter 6, such a believer is going to ultimately be ruled by the sin nature in one way or the other.

In fact, such a believer will fight against these ungodly impulses with all of his strength and power, but conclude by doing exactly what Paul also said: *"For that which I do I allow not* (I understand not): *for what I would* (walk victoriously), *that do I not; but what I hate* (to fail the Lord), *that do I"* (Rom. 7:15).

This means that no matter how hard the person struggles against sin, and the true believer will definitely struggle against sin, in such a state, that person is going to fail. Of course, we're speaking of the believer who has no knowledge of the Cross.

Now, what should be done with such a person?

PUNISHMENT?

The church, little understanding the Cross, operates on the principle of willpower and, therefore, concludes that if a Christian sins, it's simply because he has willed to sin. In other words, in the thinking of most in the church, all that Christian has to do is simply say no to sin.

They don't seem to realize that such a Christian has said no to sin untold numbers of times, but to no avail, exactly as Paul said.

So, thinking that the matter of sin is just a matter of saying yes or no, most of the time, the church operates from the position of law. In other words, the person has broken the rules, so that person must be punished.

However, there is nothing in the Word of God that speaks of one Christian punishing another. In fact, the church leaders who are doing the punishing are probably in worse shape spiritually than the one they are punishing.

The truth is, Jesus took our punishment on the tree (Gal. 3:13). For us to think that we can punish a fellow Christian, in effect, is saying that Christ wasn't punished enough, and we have to add some punishment to that which He has already suffered.

If you think about it a little bit, such an attitude borders on blasphemy!

Let me ask these questions: *What good does punishment do? How does that help a Christian get victory over his problem, whatever the problem is?*

The truth is, punishment only makes a bad matter worse. It does not help at all and, in fact, is a form of penance, which God can never accept.

SO, WHAT SHOULD BE DONE TO THE CHRISTIAN WHO SINS?

Paul told us what should be done. He said: *"Brethren, if a man be overtaken in a fault* (the word *fault* here refers to a moral failure), *you which are spiritual, restore such an one in the spirit of meekness; considering yourself, lest you also be tempted"* (Gal. 6:1).

The word *spiritual* carries the connotation of someone who understands God's prescribed order of victory, which is the Message of the Cross (I Cor. 1:17–18; 2:2, 5).

Such a believer is to tell the one who has failed the Lord, irrespective as to what the failure might be, that he has failed simply because his faith was in something other than Christ and the Cross.

In other words, the person is to be brought back to the Cross and made to understand that what Jesus did there is the source of his victory and, in fact, the only source of his victory. He is to get his faith once again in the right place, which is the Cross.

The reason for failure, and this speaks of any believer, is because our faith has been pulled from Christ and the Cross to other things. In fact, this is something that Satan relentlessly tries to do. This is why Paul also told us to *"fight the good fight of faith"* (I Tim. 6:12).

So, why is it that most so-called Christian leaders don't relay this to failing believers, preachers or otherwise?

HUMANISTIC PSYCHOLOGY AND THE CROSS

They do not relate this great truth to believers simply because they do not know and understand the truth themselves, or else, they do not believe the truth. To be frank, the greatest problem of all is not ignorance, but rather unbelief.

Have you noticed that in the last several decades, more and more, the church is directing failure to humanistic psychology? The great statement is, *"He (or she) needs professional help."* Regrettably, there is no help from that source. Not only is there no help from that source, there is actually harm from that source simply because it pulls one away from the true victory that one can have in Christ. As well, as in all error, demon spirits are involved, with the latter state of that individual being worse than at the beginning.

Sin, and sin of any stripe, is to be taken to the Cross. The Cross was brought about because of sin and is the only answer to this dread malady. For any believer, church leader or otherwise, to think that there is another solution can only be described as blasphemy!

That's exactly why Paul said: *"But though we, or an angel from heaven, preach any other gospel unto you than that which we have preached unto you, let him be accursed"* (Gal. 1:8).

This means that those who preach humanistic psychology are cursed by God, and all who come under such preaching and teaching are cursed as well.

It also means that all who subscribe to the so-called Word of Faith doctrine, which repudiates the Cross of Christ, are cursed as well.

It means also that all *"modernism"* is cursed by God simply because it denies Christ and the Cross.

OPPOSITION TO THE SACRIFICE

"And Pharaoh commanded the same day the taskmasters of the people, and their officers, saying,

"You shall no more give the people straw to make brick, as heretofore: let them go and gather straw for themselves.

"And the tale of the bricks, which they did make heretofore, you shall lay upon them; you shall not diminish ought thereof: for they be idle; therefore they cry, saying, Let us go and sacrifice to our God" (Ex. 5:6-8).

We have seen now how that God has given the demand to Pharaoh, *"Let My people go,"* but which has not been obeyed.

We now see Satan's second tactic, which is to increase the temptation, increase the pressure, and make it harder for the child of God. Hopefully, in his evil eyes, this will cause them to quit believing because of discouragement.

Oftentimes, the setting to carry out the will of God will result in Satan's anger, with opposition being increased.

Foolishly, some Christians believe that if it's the will of God, and I speak of whatever it is that we are doing, there will be no difficulties. Actually, the reverse is true. The carrying out of the will of God always brings great opposition from Satan, which should be obvious.

It is good for a man to learn painfully the nature of sin's dominion and our absolute helplessness in the grip of that monarch.

The sacrifice of an innocent animal was meant to typify the coming Son of God, who would give Himself on the Cross, which alone could break the bondage of darkness, exampled here by Pharaoh.

THE CROSS

Let the believer take a lesson from this: at the mention of sacrifice, Pharaoh increased the pressure and the workload almost to a killing pace.

This is the lesson we must learn: The Message of the Cross should be the very first thing the Christian hears after coming to Christ, but tragically, most of the time, it isn't. When he first hears the Message of the Cross and embarks upon this course, which is the only course of victory, he will find Satan greatly opposing him. The opposition will be intensified, which is meant to throw such a believer off course and actually deny the Cross.

Many Christians are confused at this point. Many get it in their minds that the Cross means that there will never be any more opposition from Satan. However, the opposition may even be intensified, possibly above anything they have heretofore experienced. When they face that opposition, many are left without understanding. This example of the children of Israel should be a lesson to us.

Satan wants you to get discouraged and to quit. He wants you to deny the Cross, which means to deny all that Christ has done for you. To do this, he will usually not lead you to deny Christ, but rather to turn your faith to something else. If he can get you to do so, he has succeeded. You will now be even tighter in his grip of bondage, with no victory on the horizon, and works of the flesh running havoc in your life.

BUT WHAT IF I FAIL?

I don't mean to be negative, but more than likely, it's *"when I fail."* In such a situation, the believer is to understand that he is the one who has failed and not the Cross. What Christ did at the Cross cannot fail. So, if there is failure, then it simply means that we have failed.

Why have we failed?

It's always a question of faith. In other words, failure, which speaks of sinning in some way, is always a failure of faith. Our faith is not as strong as we think it is, not as strong as it ought to be, and, as well, our faith may very well be turned in the wrong direction other than the Cross.

All of this is the reason that the Christian should make the Cross of Christ a daily habit. What do we mean by that?

Jesus said: *"If any man will come after Me, let him deny himself, and take up his cross daily, and follow Me"* (Lk. 9:23).

Denying oneself is not asceticism, as many believe. This particular word refers to a denial of all pleasure, etc. That's not what Jesus is speaking about here.

He is meaning that we are to deny ourselves regarding our own strength, education, motivation, ability, talent, etc., and totally and completely place our trust and faith in Christ and what Christ has done at the Cross. *"Taking up the Cross,"* refers to subscribing to its benefits, understanding that what Jesus did there is the answer to our problems.

DAILY

When he spoke of this being done on a daily basis, he was meaning that, in essence, we should begin all over again each and every day, resolving that our faith will be placed in the Cross, and believing that what Jesus did there is sufficient for all things.

To say it a better way, one should forget about what happened yesterday, and I especially speak of failure. Today is a brand-new day, and I'm going to trust God totally and completely by denying my own strength and ability and taking up the Cross. This means that I will trust totally and exclusively in what Christ did there for me. This will be my source of victory; this will be the object of my faith.

Such a believer will find himself, little by little, growing stronger and stronger, even as he begins to understand more and more the Cross and the great work accomplished there. No, the Bible doesn't teach sinless perfection, but it does teach that *"sin shall not have dominion over you"* (Rom. 6:14).

In effect, this means that the sin nature will not dominate you, will not rule over you, and will not reign in your life. Instead, you will rule and reign over it by and through the Lord Jesus Christ, trusting in what He has done for you at the Cross (Gal. 2:20–21).

INTENSIFIED OPPOSITION

"Let there more work be laid upon the men, that they may labor therein; and let them not regard vain words.

"And the taskmasters of the people went out, and their officers, and they spoke to the people, saying, Thus says Pharaoh, I will not give you straw.

"Go ye, get you straw where you can find it: yet not ought of your work shall be diminished" (Ex. 5:9-11).

Pharaoh regarded as *"vain words"* the idea of going some three days into the wilderness in order to hold a feast unto God and to offer sacrifices. Such meant nothing to him; therefore, he would ignore the request.

Not only that, he would make the lot of the people much harder than they had previously experienced.

The unbelief of Pharaoh comes out plainly here: Where God Himself is unknown, and He definitely was unknown in

Egypt, His words were, as well, but idle tales. To talk of the Cross of Christ is meaningless to the man of the world.

The Bible tells man that he is a fallen creature, unprepared to die, and unfit for the presence of a holy God. The Bible also tells him of the wondrous provision of God's grace and presents a Saviour all-sufficient for his acceptance. The Bible warns him faithfully of the solemn issues at stake and asks him how he shall escape if he neglects so great salvation. The Bible plainly tells him that he who will not believe shall be damned, and that whosoever's name is not found written in the Book of Life shall be cast into the lake of fire.

However, these solemn statements are but vain words to the skeptical heart of the natural man. He refuses to receive them as a message from the living God addressed to his own soul.

However, let him beware. Let him be warned by the awful case of Pharaoh. If he continues in his unbelief and obstinacy, Pharaoh's fate shall be his — God most certainly will bring him into judgment.

Once again we emphasize that the severe measures that Pharaoh ordered to be taken upon the Hebrews illustrate the malignant efforts of Satan against the soul that God's grace is dealing with. When the Devil recognizes the first advances of the Holy Spirit toward a poor sinner, he at once puts forth every effort to retain his victims. That goes for Christians as well!

Satan never gives up his prey without a fierce struggle. This is why so many convicted souls find that their case gets worse before it is bettered. So it was here with the Hebrews.

Just as hope was awakened, the opposition against them became stronger. Just when deliverance seemed nigh, their oppression was increased.

THE TASKMASTERS

"So the people were scattered abroad throughout all the land of Egypt to gather stubble instead of straw.

"And the taskmasters hasted them, saying, Fulfill your works, your daily tasks, as when there was straw.

"And the officers of the children of Israel, which Pharaoh's taskmasters had set over them, were beaten, and demanded, Wherefore have you not fulfilled your task in making brick both yesterday and today, as heretofore?" (Ex. 5:12-14).

Satan's plan was to make the hardships of the children of Israel harder yet, and to do so to such an extent that they would want to drop all ideas of leaving Egypt, if Pharaoh would only lessen the pressure and allow them to again be as they once were. In other words, Satan wanted them to be willing to remain as slaves in Egypt. He almost succeeded!

Let me say it again: The moment you as the believer hear the great Message of the Cross and what it can do in your heart and life, if you truly love the Lord, you will realize that what you are hearing is truth, and your spirit will immediately tell you so. However, then Satan begins to come against you in full force, perhaps even stronger than ever before. He doesn't want you to know and have the deliverance that the Cross alone can bring. So, he opposes with all the strength of hell.

Sometimes his taskmasters will be so-called fellow believers. They will try to dissuade you and discourage you, and will try to make you believe something other than the truth. Then they will load you down with guilt because the government of law is being abandoned, with the government of grace being accepted.

TOTAL COMMITMENT

When one accepts the Message of the Cross, one soon begins to find that this involves every aspect of his faith and believing. Much to his dismay, he will find that most of the church world is operating in another direction. In other words, what is being done is not scriptural. Consequently, that person might even have to leave his church because they are not preaching the Cross. As well, family and friends may have to be laid aside simply because this message pertains itself to a complete lifestyle. Everything comes under the scrutiny of the Cross, and as a result, many feel that it's too difficult, too hard.

As stated, the taskmasters will more than likely be those who are of one's own rank, but the truth is, they are *"Egyptians!"*

The Cross of Christ addresses everything in a person's life, holding back nothing. It shows our efforts of the flesh to be just that, worthless! It exposes all of our works, religion, and everything that doesn't line up with the Word of God. That's what angers people, especially religious people.

THE SACRIFICE TO THE LORD

"Then the officers of the children of Israel came and cried unto Pharaoh, saying, Wherefore deal you thus with your servants?

"There is no straw given unto your servants, and they say to us, Make brick: and, behold, your servants are beaten; but the fault is in your own people.

"But he said, You are idle, you are idle: therefore you say, Let us go and do sacrifice to the LORD.

"Go therefore now, and work; for there shall no straw be given you, yet shall you deliver the tale of bricks." (Ex. 5:15-18).

It is the *sacrifice* that rankled Pharaoh, even though he would not have been totally aware as to exactly what it all meant.

Regarding this grave problem, the Scripture says that the officers of the children of Israel came and cried unto Pharaoh.

Why didn't they go to the Lord? Tragically, God is generally our last resource! Deeply humbling is this! Amazing is the grace that bears with such waywardness. Grace not only has to begin the work of salvation, but it also has to continue and complete it. It is all of grace from first to last, or else, we wouldn't be here.

Little good it did for Israel's officers to appeal to Pharaoh, and little good it will do to appeal to man in any case.

UNBELIEF

Our dependence, our trust, and our faith must always and without exception be in the Lord. We must take everything to the Lord in prayer, realizing that He alone can bring about what is needed. He has the power to do so, and He is willing and able to do so.

So, why is it that we go to Pharaoh instead of the Lord?

The greatest problem, more than likely, is unbelief. In fact, most modern Christians have very little relationship with the Lord. As such, there is very little faith and confidence in Him. As well, I firmly believe that the major reason for this is a lack of understanding of the Cross of Christ. Not understanding the finished work, one really doesn't understand Christ. As a result, faith is placed elsewhere, and I might quickly add, it gets the same results as the children of Israel did with Pharaoh.

This is not meant to say that we are to eliminate all human contact. That's not the idea. In fact, we have to work with individuals, and at times, ask help from individuals. However, everything must be soaked in prayer, knowing that God is able to maneuver the situation to where we will receive the help we need, whatever way it comes.

In denominations, the truth is, these organizations are at least as political, and perhaps even more political, than politics itself. It's the old, *"I'll scratch your back if you'll scratch mine"* syndrome. It's people pulling strings and manipulating other people, all to try to get them to do what one wants done.

Once you're out of such, and you look back at the situation, it becomes sickening. It portrays people who claim the Lord but, in reality, have precious little confidence in the Lord, if any at all. They are trusting in themselves or other men, and while they claim trust in the Lord, their actions prove otherwise.

We should learn that it's not scriptural for us to make plans and then ask God to bless those plans. If God makes the plans, they are assured of blessing. So, leave Pharaoh alone and depend exclusively on the Lord for all that is done.

THE COMPLAINT OF THE PEOPLE

"And the officers of the children of Israel did see that they were in evil case, after it was said, You shall not minish ought from your bricks of your daily task.

"And they met Moses and Aaron, who stood in the way, as they came forth from Pharaoh:

"And they said unto them, The LORD look upon you, and judge; because you have made our savour to be abhorred in the eyes of Pharaoh, and in the eyes of his servants, to put a sword in their hand to slay us" (Ex. 5:19-21).

God had said, *"Let My people go,"* but Pharaoh ignored what was said. To be sure, the great word, *Let My people go,* has gone out regarding His church, but that doesn't mean that Pharaoh is going to fold and buckle.

The Evil One will undoubtedly make the temptation even harder and make the pressure even more powerful, in other words, do everything he can to discourage you. He wants you to abandon the Cross and go elsewhere.

So, you must expect Satan to do his worst, but he is doing such because he knows that you have at last heard the truth, and if you do not fold, victory will be yours. He knows all of this!

Now the elders of the children of Israel turned against Moses and Aaron. This was perhaps the hardest cut of all. To be sure, your family may turn against you, your closest friends may turn against you, and you may have to leave the church where you are now attending, and your family has attended there for all of your life. Religious people love the religion of works. When something is proposed that strikes that down, that exposes it for what it is, and they don't want to hear about it. So, you might have problems in that capacity as well.

The effort of a child of God to walk in victory, with his or her faith exclusively in the Cross, is often chilled by similar unbelief on the part of the church and by opposition on the part of the world.

The people now criticized Moses and, in essence, through Moses, criticized the Lord.

Moses was, no doubt, prepared for the rebuff that he had himself received from Pharaoh, for the Lord had plainly said that He would harden the king's heart. However, so far as the inspired record informs us, nothing had been told him that he would meet with discouragement and opposition from his own brethren. A real testing was this for God's servant, for it is far more trying to be criticized by our own, by those whom we are anxious to help, than it is to be persecuted by the world.

However, it is sufficient for the servant to be as his master. The Lord Himself was hated by His own brethren according to the flesh, and the very ones to whom He had ministered in ceaseless grace unanimously cried, *"Crucify Him."*

THE LORD

"And Moses returned unto the LORD*, and said,* LORD*, wherefore have You so evil entreated this people? why is it that You have sent me?*

"For since I came to Pharaoh to speak in Your name, he has done evil to this people; neither have You delivered Your people at all" (Ex. 5:22-23).

We may well question how far genuine faith, or a mortified will, dictated the *"wherefore"* and the *"why"* of Moses in the above quotation. Still, the Lord did not rebuke a remonstrance drawn forth by the intense pressure of the moment. By contrast, the Lord graciously replied to Moses.

To Moses' credit, he did take his problem to the Lord, even though his words were not exactly faith-filled.

We erroneously tend to think that when the Lord is about to do something for us, everything will suddenly smooth out, all the pieces expertly fall into place, and everything seem to function exactly as it ought to function.

It is seldom that way, however! It should be understood that Satan doesn't desire the Lord to do anything for anyone. Whenever a saint of God begins to believe God for something, the Evil One then seeks to hinder, and to hinder greatly, this which the Lord is about to do. He tries to get the believer to grow discouraged, to complain, and, hopefully, to quit.

So, in essence, all of this boils down, so to speak, to the three following particulars:

1. The Lord has given the command through His Word, actually, the Message of the Cross, for you to be free, but just because the Lord has given the Word, it doesn't mean that Satan is going to back down.

2. Knowing that you have received the truth, actually the truth that will set you free, Satan will very likely increase the pressure and increase the temptation, all to discourage you so that you will throw it over and quit. In other words, he wants you to say, *"Well, the Cross may work for other people, but it doesn't work for me,"* etc. Let's always remember this: The Cross always works. It's you and me who have the problem doing what we need to do. Please understand, if you fail, get back up and get your faith right, and the Lord will help you on your way. This I guarantee: victory will ultimately be yours.

3. As we saw, Moses had the elders of Israel to turn against him. As stated, this probably was the worst cut of all. Likewise, you may have the same problem with your family, your friends, your loved ones, and even your church.

Now, that's what the Lord gave me that Saturday night several years ago, and now that you know Satan's tactics, you'll be far more able to hold your ground. Remember this, the Holy Spirit through Paul said, *"sin shall not have dominion over you"* (Rom. 6:14).

"Yield not to temptation, for yielding is sin;
"Each victory will help you some other to win;
"Fight manfully onward, dark passions subdue,
"Look ever to Jesus, He'll carry you through."

"Shun evil companions, bad language disdain,
"God's name hold in reverence, nor take it in vain;
"Be thoughtful and earnest, kindhearted and true,
"Look ever to Jesus, He'll carry you through."

"To him who overcomes God gives a crown,
"Through faith we shall conquer, tho' often cast down;
"He who is our Saviour, our strength will renew,
"Look ever to Jesus, He'll carry you through."

BIBLIOGRAPHY

CHAPTER 1

C.H. Mackintosh, *Notes on the Book of Exodus*, New York, Loizeaux Brothers, 1880, pg. 2.

C.H. Mackintosh, *Notes on the Book of Exodus*, New York, Loizeaux Brothers, 1880, pg. 6.

H.D.M. Spence, *The Pulpit Commentary: Exodus 1:13*, Grand Rapids, Eerdmans Publishing Company, 1978.

C.H. Mackintosh, *Notes on the Book of Exodus*, New York, Loizeaux Brothers, 1880, pg. 7

CHAPTER 2

Ellicott's Commentary on the Whole Bible, Zondervan Publishing House, New York, 1880, pg. 195.

Arthur W. Pink, *Gleanings in Exodus*, Sovereign Grace Publishers, Lafayette, 2002, pg. 16.

Ibid., pg. 16.

George Williams, *William's Complete Bible Commentary,* Grand Rapids, Kregel Publications, 1994, pg. 44.

Arthur W. Pink, *Gleanings in Exodus,* Sovereign Grace Publishers, Lafayette, 2002, pg. 17.

CHAPTER 3

Arthur W. Pink, *Gleanings in Exodus,* Sovereign Grace Publishers, Lafayette, 2002, pg. 25.

Ibid., pg. 25.

Matthew Henry, *Matthew Henry's Commentary on the Whole Bible: Exodus 3:7-10,* Hendrickson Publishers, Inc., 1994.

Arthur W. Pink, *Gleanings in Exodus,* Sovereign Grace Publishers, Lafayette, 2002, pg. 29.

Ibid., pg. 29.

C.H. Mackintosh, *Notes on the Book of Exodus,* New York, Loizeaux Brothers, 1880, pg. 57.

CHAPTER 4

C.H. Mackintosh, Notes on the Book of Exodus, New York, Loizeaux Brothers, 1880, pg. 58.

George Williams, *William's Complete Bible Commentary,* Grand Rapids, Kregel Publications, 1994 , pg. 46.

H.D.M. Spence, *The Pulpit Commentary: Exodus 4:11-13,* Grand Rapids, Eerdmans Publishing Company, 1978.

C.H. Mackintosh, *Notes on the Book of Exodus,* New York, Loizeaux Brothers, 1880, pg. 64.

George Williams, *William's Complete Bible Commentary,* Grand Rapids, Kregel Publications, 1994, pg. 46.

Ibid., pg. 46.

H.D.M. Spence, *The Pulpit Commentary: Exodus 4:21,* Grand Rapids, Eerdmans Publishing Company, 1978.

George Williams, *William's Complete Bible Commentary,* Grand Rapids, Kregel Publications, 1994 , Pg. 47.

Ibid., pg 47.

CHAPTER 5

Arthur W. Pink, *Gleanings in Exodus,* Sovereign Grace Publishers, Lafayette, 2002, Pg. 42.

Ibid., pg. 42.

Ibid., pg. 42.

C.H. Mackintosh, *Notes on the Book of Exodus,* New York, Loizeaux Brothers, 1880, pg. 79.

ABOUT EVANGELIST JIMMY SWAGGART

The Rev. Jimmy Swaggart is a Pentecostal evangelist whose anointed preaching and teaching has drawn multitudes to the Cross of Christ since 1956.

As an author, he has written more than 50 books, commentaries, study guides, and The Expositor's Study Bible, which has sold nearly 2 million copies.

As an award-winning musician and singer, Brother Swaggart has recorded more than 50 gospel albums and sold nearly 16 million recordings worldwide.

For nearly six decades, Brother Swaggart has channeled his preaching and music ministry through multiple media venues including print, radio, television and the Internet.

In 2010, Jimmy Swaggart Ministries launched its own cable channel, SonLife Broadcasting Network, which airs 24 hours a day to a potential viewing audience of more than 1 billion people around the globe.

Brother Swaggart also pastors Family Worship Center in Baton Rouge, Louisiana, the church home and headquarters of Jimmy Swaggart Ministries.

Jimmy Swaggart Ministries materials can be found at **www.jsm.org**.

NOTES

NOTES

NOTES